Social Issues in Literature

Power in William Shakespeare's *Macbeth*

Other Books in the Social Issues in Literature Series:

Depression in J.D. Salinger's *Catcher in the Rye*

Industrialism in John Steinbeck's *The Grapes of Wrath*

Issues of Class in Jane Austen's *Pride and Prejudice*

Male/Female Roles in Ernest Hemingway's *The Sun Also Rises*

Political Issues in J.K. Rowling's Harry Potter Series

Racism in *The Autobiography of Malcolm X*

Suicide in Arthur Miller's *Death of a Salesman*

Women's Issues in Nathaniel Hawthorne's *The Scarlet Letter*

Worker's Rights in Upton Sinclair's *The Jungle*

Social Issues
in Literature

Power in William Shakespeare's *Macbeth*

Vernon Elso Johnson, Book Editor

GREENHAVEN PRESS
A part of Gale, Cengage Learning

Detroit • New York • San Francisco • New Haven, Conn • Waterville, Maine • London

Christine Nasso, *Publisher*
Elizabeth Des Chenes, *Managing Editor*

For more information, contact:
Greenhaven Press
27500 Drake Rd.
Farmington Hills, MI 48331-3535
Or you can visit our Internet site at gale.cengage.com

Articles in Greenhaven Press anthologies are often edited for length to meet page requirements. In addition, original titles of these works are changed to clearly present the main thesis and to explicitly indicate the author's opinion. Every effort is made to ensure that Greenhaven Press accurately reflects the original intent of the authors. Every effort has been made to trace the owners of copyrighted material.

LIBRARY OF CONGRESS CATALOGING-IN-PUBLICATION DATA

Power in William Shakespeare's Macbeth / Vernon Elso Johnson, book editor.
p. cm. -- (Social issues in literature)
Includes bibliographical references and index.
ISBN 978-0-7377-4398-2
ISBN 978-0-7377-4397-5 (pbk.)
1. Shakespeare, William, 1564-1616 Macbeth. 2. Power (Social sciences) in literature. I. Johnson, Vernon E. (Vernon Elso), 1921-
PR2823.P75 2009
822.3'3--dc22

2008050585

Printed in the United States of America
1 2 3 4 5 6 7 13 12 11 10 09

Contents

Introduction

On Wednesday, April 9, 2008, Maureen Dowd's column about congressional hearings on Iraq appeared in the *New York Times.* It was titled "Toil and Trouble," words from the witches' chants in Shakespeare's *Macbeth.* More than four hundred years after *Macbeth* first appeared on stage, a writer for America's leading newspaper used Shakespeare's story of a man's insatiable hunger for power to explore power in twenty-first-century politics.

For four hundred years Macbeth has been held up on the stage and in the classroom as a hero of great sensitivity and poetry. Yet he is a murderer from a savage time, who can march through blood and rip open the bodies of his enemies to raise his status and increase his power. When he is first introduced to the witches' prophecy that he will be king, his mind leaps to fulfillment. He holds our sympathy in part because of an early glimpse of conscience, however weak, in a terrifying moment, as he is goaded by his wife to kill the king. But afterward, he is a killer-tyrant with a single purpose: to eliminate anyone who might challenge his power. In the process, he murders not only the king, but others who threaten his throne, including an innocent woman and her son.

Macbeth was written against a backdrop of attempted plots to gain and keep power. The reign of Shakespeare's sovereign, Queen Elizabeth, began with tumultuous struggles over who should occupy the throne of England after the death of her father, Henry VIII. Edward, her sickly brother, ascended the throne at nine years old, and Elizabeth was falsely rumored to have had a part in her uncle's plot to overthrow her brother. The Boy King died in 1553, and Elizabeth's half sister, known as Bloody Mary, became queen. Mary and her devotees were convinced that Elizabeth was part of another conspiracy to take the throne, so Mary imprisoned Elizabeth in the Tower of

London. After Mary's death in 1558, Elizabeth took the throne. Elizabeth was convinced that another Mary—her cousin, Mary, Queen of Scots—was a threat to her position. When Mary, Queen of Scots, was usurped by Scottish noblemen, she fled to London for Elizabeth's protection, not knowing that Elizabeth was supporting Mary's enemies. Mary was imprisoned, found by the court to be part of the Babington plot in 1586 to murder the queen, and was executed as a traitor.

Thirteen years later, another plot against Elizabeth was launched when one of the queen's favorites, the second Earl of Essex, tried to incite the general populace to revolt against Elizabeth. He was arrested and executed.

In 1588, Elizabeth's throne was again threatened, this time by Philip of Spain, but the English defeated the vaunted Spanish Armada that Philip sent against them.

At Elizabeth's death in 1603, James VI of Scotland, the son of Mary, Queen of Scots, became King James I of England. He was a great admirer of Shakespeare, whose plays were performed at court. But James's reign was also plagued by treason and bloodshed. In 1605, when Shakespeare was forty-one years old, fourteen pro-Catholic conspirators tried to blow up Parliament and the king. Guards found the bomb expert, Guy Fawkes, in the cellar of the House of Lords with thirty-six barrels of gunpowder. In 1606, after this event, known as the Gunpowder Plot, Shakespeare's *Macbeth* was performed on stage.

As intrigue and bloodshed in the fanatical quest for power formed the political background of Shakespeare's life and history, so from his earliest plays in 1590, Shakespeare was fixated with the idea of upheavals in the state from those driven to grab and hold supremacy. Before composing *Macbeth*, Shakespeare had written thirteen plays—histories and tragedies—on the issue, most of which contained elements that surfaced again in *Macbeth*. Chief of these elements was the usurpation or attempted usurpation of the power of the ruler,

William Shakespeare. The Library of Congress. Reproduced by permission.

as in the Henry plays, *Richard the Third, Julius Caesar, King Lear*, and *Hamlet*. A common action is the betrayal of friends and even brothers, parents, and children, as in the case of *Hamlet* and *King Lear*. There are also horrific murders, often of innocents. In *Richard III*, as in *Macbeth*, children are slaughtered in a monster's attempt to gain the throne and keep it. In several plays, including the Henry plays and *Hamlet*, that which is seemingly supernatural plays a role in either ambition or revenge, as do ambitious women, hungry for control or exalted rank for the men in their lives (and, of course, themselves).

Although achieving and maintaining power is central to the play, it is not a simple issue, as the following essays illustrate. Critics raise the following questions: Is Macbeth merely upholding the military "virtues" he was trained to value? Do the opposing Christian virtues play any part in Macbeth's character? Does Macbeth ever really atone for his murders? Does he bear full responsibility for his acts or is he, in some respects, a victim, manipulated by the witches and his wife? Why do we sympathize with this murderous traitor? Is it because Shakespeare puts powerful and moving words in his mouth?

The final essays in this volume illustrate just how persistent and enduring the theme of power has been, and is, in the modern world. There are tyrants, who, like Macbeth, have killed to gain the seat of power in their countries and, like Macbeth, have murdered to keep power in their own hands. Sometimes democracy itself is the victim and, in the United States, some observers feel that the executive branch of the government has been accruing more and more authority, destroying the constitutionally mandated balance between the executive, legislative, and judicial branches. The final essay examines the misuse of power by big businesses' chief executive officers, who have, the author asserts, become the new kings of American society.

The critics included here cover a hundred years of scholarship and offer a wide range of views on *Macbeth*, while current viewpoints illustrate that a Macbeth-like lust for power still haunts our world.

Chronology

1558
Elizabeth I ascends the throne.

1564
William Shakespeare is born at Stratford-upon-Avon.

1567
In Scotland, Mary Queen of Scots is deposed and eleven-month-old James VI ascends the throne.

1568
John Shakespeare, Shakespeare's father, is elected bailiff, but rumors that he is secretly a Catholic damage his standing in the community.

1570
Elizabeth is excommunicated by Pope Paul V.

1576
The Theatre (the first professional theater) opens in the north of London.

1579
Jesuits begin missions to England.

1581
Strong anti-Catholic laws are passed.

1582
William Shakespeare marries Anne Hathaway.

1583
Shakespeare's daughter Susanna is born.
Catholics by the thousands are persecuted, jailed, or killed.

1585
Shakespeare's twins, Hamnet and Judith, are born.

1587
Mary Queen of Scots is executed for conspiring against Elizabeth. Pope Sixtus V begins a crusade against England.

1588–1589
Shakespeare goes to London without his family. His first plays are performed.

1590–1592
The Comedy of Errors and three parts of *Henry VI* are presented.

1593
London is hit by the plague, closing theaters.

1593–1594
Shakespeare acquires a share in the Lord Chamberlain's Men, beginning a successful career as an investor in theaters.
Venus and Adonis and *The Rape of Lucrece* are published and *The Taming of the Shrew*, *Two Gentlemen of Verona*, and *Richard the III* are performed.

1595–1596
Romeo and Juliet, Richard the II, King John, A Midsummer Night's Dream, and *Love's Labours Lost* are produced.

1596
Hamnet dies; Shakespeare's father is granted a coat of arms.

1597
The Merchant of Venice and *Henry IV, Part I* are produced, and Shakespeare invests in property in Stratford.
King James VI of Scotland publishes a tract on witchcraft titled *Daemonologie.*

1598–1600

As You Like It, Much Ado About Nothing, The Merry Wives of Windsor, Henry V, Henry IV, Part 2, and *Julius Caesar* are presented. Shakespeare's company moves to the Globe Theatre.

1601

The Earl of Essex is executed in the Tower of London after a failed attempt to take over the throne, which creates great anxiety within Shakespeare's company.

Shakespeare's father dies after much trouble and investigation as a possible secret Catholic.

1602

Twelfth Night is produced.

1603

Elizabeth dies, and James VI of Scotland ascends the English throne as James I. He is a scholar, an expert on witchcraft, and a believer in the divine right of kings.

Shakespeare's company becomes the King's Men.

1604

Measure for Measure and *Othello* are produced.

1605

The Gunpowder Plot (planned by Catholics) against King James I and Parliament is discovered, resulting in panic and the persecution of Catholics.

1605–1606

King Lear is produced, and *Macbeth* is presumably presented before James I.

1606–1608

Pericles is performed at court. *Antony and Cleopatra, Coriolanus, The Winter's Tale*, and *Cymbeline* are produced.

1608
Shakespeare's mother, Mary Arden, dies.

1609
Shakespeare's company purchases Blackfriars Theatre.

1610–1611
The Tempest is produced, and Shakespeare moves to Stratford.

1613
Henry VIII is produced; the Globe is destroyed by fire, but reopens the following year.

1616
Shakespeare dies.

1623
The first Folio edition of Shakespeare's works is published (including the first printing of *Macbeth*).

Social Issues in Literature

Chapter 1

Background on William Shakespeare

Shakespeare and His Times

John F. Andrews

John F. Andrews, the author of many books and articles on Shakespeare, is founder and CEO of the Shakespeare Guild, former editor of Shakespeare Quarterly, *and former executive director of the Washington, D.C., branch of the English-Speaking Union.*

In the following selection, John F. Andrews examines Shakespeare's schooling, family life, and burgeoning career, as well as the career of his father, John, whose rising social standing had allowed access to a fully classical education for his eldest son. Andrews describes the city of London as it was at the time of Shakespeare's appearance there in the early 1590s as a member of the acting troupe the Lord Chamberlain's Men. Andrews also discusses Shakespeare's use of the so-called Tudor myth in his historical works. The Tudor myth is the idea that although God had punished England for its bloody power conflicts (such as that dramatized in Macbeth*), after the accession to the throne in 1485 of the first Tudor, Henry VII, God favored England—a favor confirmed by the stunning defeat of the Spanish Armada by the English in 1588.*

If Shakespeare was a man for all time, he was also very much a man of his own age. Christened at Holy Trinity Church in Stratford-upon-Avon on 26 April 1564, he grew up as the eldest of five children reared by John Shakespeare, a tradesman who played an increasingly active role in the town's civic affairs as his business prospered, and Mary Arden Shakespeare, the daughter of a gentleman farmer from nearby Wilmcote. Whether Shakespeare was born on 23 April, as tradition holds, is not known; but a birth date only a few days prior to the recorded baptism seems eminently probable, particularly in view of the fear his parents must have had that William, like two sisters who had preceded him and one who followed, might die in infancy. By the time young William was old enough to begin attending school, he had a younger brother (Gilbert, born in 1566) and a baby sister (Joan, born in 1569). As he attained his youth, he found himself with two more brothers to help look after (Richard, born in 1574, and Edmund, born in 1580), the younger of whom eventually followed his by-then-prominent eldest brother to London and the theater, where he had a brief career as an actor before his untimely death at twenty-seven. . . .

Shakespeare's Father

Even if John Shakespeare was not one of the "learned," he was certainly a man of what a later age would call upward mobility. By marrying Mary Arden, the daughter of his father's landlord, he acquired the benefits of a better social standing and a lucrative inheritance, much of which he invested in property (he bought several houses). And by involving himself in public service, he rose by sure degrees to the highest municipal positions Stratford had to offer: chamberlain (1561), alderman (1565), and bailiff (or mayor) and justice of the peace (1568). A few years after his elevation to the office of bailiff, probably around 1576, John Shakespeare approached the College of Heralds for armorial bearings and the right to call himself a gentleman. Before his application was acted upon, however, his fortunes took a sudden turn for the worse, and it was not until 1596, when his eldest son had attained some status and renewed the petition, that a Shakespeare coat of arms was finally granted. This must have been a comfort to John Shakespeare in his declining years (he died in 1601), because by then he had borrowed money, disposed of property out of necessity, ceased to attend meetings of the town council, become involved in litigation and been assessed fines, and even stopped attending church services, for fear, it was said, "of process for debt." Just what happened to alter John Shakespeare's financial and social position after the mid 1570s is not clear. Some have seen his nonattendance at church as a sign that he had become a recusant, unwilling to conform to the practices of the newly established Church of England (his wife's family had remained loyal to Roman Catholicism despite the fact that the old faith was under vigorous attack in Warwickshire [Stratford's county] after 1577), but the scant surviving evidence is anything but definitive. . . .

Schooling and Marriage

Given his father's social position, young William would have been eligible to attend the King's New School, located above the Guild Hall and adjacent to the Guild Chapel (institutions that would both have been quite familiar to a man with the elder Shakespeare's municipal duties), no more than a five-minute walk from the Shakespeare house on Henley Street. Though no records survive to tell us who attended the Stratford grammar school during this period, we do know that it had well-qualified and comparatively well-paid masters; and, through the painstaking research of such scholars as T. W. Baldwin, we now recognize that a curriculum such as the one offered at the King's New School would have equipped its pupils with what by modern standards would be a rather formidable classical education.

During his many long school days there, young Shakespeare would have become thoroughly grounded in Latin, acquired some background in Greek, and developed enough linguistic facility to pick up whatever he may have wanted later from such modern languages as Italian and French. . . .

Once his school years ended, Shakespeare married, at eighteen, a woman who was eight years his senior. We know that

Anne Hathaway was pregnant when the marriage license was issued by the Bishop of Worcester on 27 November 1582, because a daughter, Susanna, was baptized in Holy Trinity six months later on 26 May 1583. . . .

Shakespeare in London

Shakespeare probably traveled the hundred miles to London by way of the spires of Oxford, as do most visitors returning from Stratford to London today. But why he went, or when, history does not tell us. It has been plausibly suggested that he joined an acting troupe (the Queen's Men) that was one player short when it toured Stratford in 1587. If so, he may have migrated by way of one or two intermediary companies to a position with the troupe that became the Lord Chamberlain's Men in 1594. The only thing we can assert with any assurance is that by 1592 Shakespeare had established himself as an actor and had written at least three plays. . . .

If we look at what Shakespeare had written by the early 1590s, we see that he had already become thoroughly familiar with the daily round of one of the great capitals of Europe. Shakespeare knew St. Paul's Cathedral, famous not only as a house of worship but also as the marketplace where books were bought and sold. He knew the Inns of Court, where aspiring young lawyers studied for the bar. He knew the river Thames, spanned by the ever-busy, ever-fascinating London Bridge. He knew the Tower, where so many of the characters he would depict in his history plays had met their deaths, and where in his own lifetime such prominent noblemen as the Earl of Essex and Sir Walter Raleigh would be imprisoned prior to their executions. He knew Westminster, where Parliament met when summoned by the Queen, and where the Queen herself held court at Whitehall Palace. He knew the harbor, where English ships, having won control of the seas by defeating the "invincible" Spanish Armada in 1588, had begun in earnest to explore the New World. . . .

Tudor-style building, Shakespeare's birthplace, Stratford-upon-Avon, England. Copyright © 2006 Kelly A. Quin.

The Lord Chamberlain's Men

One gathers . . . that, like other playwrights of the period, Shakespeare was careful not to refer too overtly to deficiencies in the well-to-do members of his audiences, especially when such members might include the nobility or persons close to them. After all, an acting company's livelihood depended upon its securing and retaining favor at Court—not only because of the extra income and prestige that accrued from periodic Court performances commissioned by the Master of the Revels, but even more fundamentally because a company could perform in or near London only if it were licensed to do so by the Crown and enjoyed the protection of a noble or royal patron. A prudent playwright would not wish to jeopardize his company's standing with the monarch. And Shakespeare and his colleagues—the other "sharers" who owned stock in the company that was known as the Lord Chamberlain's Men from 1594 until 1603 (when Queen Elizabeth died and was succeeded by King James I) and the King's Men thereafter (having received a patent as the new monarch's own players)—must have been prudent, because theirs was by far the most prosperous and the most frequently "preferred" theatrical organization in the land, from its inception in the early 1590s until the triumph of Puritanism finally brought about the closing of the theaters half a century later in 1642.

Shakespeare's position with the Lord Chamberlain's Men was a source of professional stability that probably had a great deal to do with his growth and maturation as a writer. For one thing, it freed him from some of the uncertainties and frustrations that must have been the lot of other playwrights, virtually all of whom operated as free-lancers selling their wares to impresarios such as Philip Henslowe (often for as little as five pounds), and most of whom thus forfeited any real say about how their plays were to be produced and, in time (if a given acting company so wished or if chance provided), published. From at least 1594 on Shakespeare was a stockholder of the theatrical organization for which he wrote his plays. After 1598 (when the sons of the recently deceased James Burbage, Cuthbert and Richard, invited four of the principal actors in the Lord Chamberlain's Men to become their partners and put up half the capital needed to rebuild the Theatre across the Thames as the Globe), Shakespeare was also a co-owner of the playhouse in which that company performed the plays. As such, he shared in all the profits the Lord Chamberlain's Men took in at the gate, and he was undoubtedly a participant in most, if not all, of the major decisions affecting the company's welfare. We know from the surviving legal records of the playwright's various business transactions that he prospered financially by this arrangement: like his father, Shakespeare invested wisely in real estate, purchasing properties in both Stratford and London. And we can infer from the evidence of his rapidly developing sophistication as a dramatist that Shakespeare's membership in a close-knit group of theatrical entrepreneurs also helped him flourish artistically. . . .

Like his fellow playwrights when they donned personae as men of letters, Shakespeare was addressing his efforts, first of all, to a noble patron and, second, to a cultivated readership. He was therefore concerned that his compositions be published as he had written them, and he took pains to assure that they were accompanied by a graceful appeal for the approval of an audience presumed to embody the highest standards of literary taste and judgment. . . .

England and Her Kings

[In discussing] his two decades as a playwright, we should probably begin where scholars now think he himself began: as the principal practitioner, if not in many ways the originator, of a new kind of drama that sprang from native patriotism. The most immediate "source" of the English history play appears to have been the heightened sense of national destiny that came in the wake of the royal navy's seemingly providential victory over the Spanish Armada in 1588. Proud of the new eminence their nation had achieved, and immensely relieved that the threat of invasion by a Catholic power had been averted, many of Shakespeare's contemporaries were disposed to view England's deliverance as a sign of heaven's favor. . . .

Given this context, it must have seemed entirely fitting that sometime in the late 1580s or early 1590s an enterprising young playwright began dramatizing a sequence of historical developments that were almost universally regarded as the "roots" of England's current greatness. . . . Here [Shakespeare] also found a theological reading of political history that treated England as a collective Everyman—falling into sin, undergoing a terrifyingly bloody punishment for its disobedience, and eventually finding its way back to redemption through the emergence of Henry VII.

The chances are that as Shakespeare matured in his craft he came to view the "Tudor myth" (as E. M. W. Tillyard has termed this official dogma) with a degree of skeptical detachment; but even so, he seems to have found in its clear, broad sweep a pattern that served quite well as a way of organizing the disparate materials he chose to dramatize.

Shakespeare's Path to Success

Peter Holland

Peter Holland is McMeel Family Professor of Shakespearean Studies at the University of Notre Dame. A specialist in Shakespeare in performance, he is a prominent editor of Shakespearean studies.

In the following selection, Peter Holland describes Shakespeare's path to success in the London theater. In Stratford in 1587, Shakespeare might have joined the Queen's Men, a company that presented plays that clearly influenced Shakespeare's earlier works. The company needed an extra actor at that time, but the connection is murky, as are theatrical records of the London theater during the plague years. By 1594, Holland explains, Shakespeare was with the Lord Chamberlain's Men, had written several plays, and was a shareholder in a stock company of actors, all of which secured his income, his status, and his reputation at the court of Queen Elizabeth I.

When Shakespeare became a player [actor] is not clear but it is at least possible that he joined the [acting troupe known as the] Queen's Men. They played in Stratford in 1587 and their repertory included a play based on Montemayor's *Diana* (the source for Shakespeare's *The Two Gentlemen of Verona*), anonymous plays on the reigns of King John (*The Troublesome Reign*), Richard III (*The True Tragedy*), Henry IV, and Henry V (both covered by *The Famous Victories of Henry V*), all subjects of plays by Shakespeare himself in the 1590s, as well as *King Leir* which, as well as being the major source for Shakespeare's *King Lear*, has possibly left its trace-

Peter Holland, "Shakespeare, William," *Oxford Dictionary of National Biography*. Vol. 49. Edited by H.C.G. Matthew and Brian Harrison. Oxford: Oxford University Press, 2004.

on a number of his earlier works. Though he was influenced by many other plays, not least the work of Christopher Marlowe, in developing his own style in his early works, there is no comparable body of sustained influence. If not actually in the Queen's Men, he certainly seems to have known their work especially well and the plays that belonged to them were crucial to Shakespeare's histories, the works that established the Lord Chamberlain's Men as the pre-eminent company of the age. The Queen's Men's works were virulently anti-Catholic and the company may even have owed its existence to a political aim of touring anti-Catholic propaganda; Shakespeare's plays that owe something of their existence to the Queen's Men's repertory, while hardly being Catholic apologetics, are strikingly less factional in their religion. . . .

The Lord Chamberlain's Men

Before the plague most of Shakespeare's plays were probably written for and sold to Lord Strange's Men, later the Earl of Derby's Men, though *2* and *3 Henry VI* and possibly *The Taming of the Shrew* were performed by Pembroke's Men, a company which flourished briefly in London between 1591 and 1593. If one notes the prominence of Lord Stanley, the Earl of Derby, in *Richard III*, then it may be a careful compliment to the current earl of Derby as the players' patron; if one sees the character as a perfect time-server who does his best to stay out of the battle until he can align himself with the winning side, then it may be rather less of a compliment. *Richard III* may be the last play Shakespeare wrote with Strange's Men in mind.

The effect of plague and the difficulty of making a profit by touring affected all the playing companies. The history of the theatre companies in London, their repertory and resources in this period, is as murky as much else to do with Shakespeare's life. *Titus Andronicus*, for instance, was performed by the three different companies named on the title-page of its first printing in 1594: Derby's (that is, Lord Strange's Men), Pembroke's, and Sussex's players; but it could have been either by each successively or by a company containing members of all three. But in May 1594 Henry Carey, Lord Hunsdon, who was lord chamberlain, and his son-in-law Charles, Lord Howard, the lord admiral and previous lord chamberlain, created something approaching a duopoly for their players in London. . . .

Hunsdon's Men, now known as the Lord Chamberlain's Men, including some of the best actors of Derby's and Pembroke's companies, played at The Theatre to the north-east of the city, beginning their long and unequalled period as the greatest company of actors in the country.

From this point on all Shakespeare's new plays were written for and belonged to the Lord Chamberlain's Men. What is more, payments to the company for their court performances over the Christmas season of 1594 name Shakespeare with William Kemp, the company's clown, and Richard Burbage, their leading actor, as the three payees, indicating their pre-eminent status among the small group of sharers in the company. Though often called actor-sharers, the participants in the Chamberlain's Men were unlikely to have included Shakespeare on the grounds of his acting ability. Uniquely among playwrights of the period, Shakespeare began a long and uninterrupted association with and participation in one particular theatre company, rather than, as it were, accepting freelance work for whoever would pay. Though later dramatists like John Fletcher, Philip Massinger, Richard Brome, and James Shirley had similar links to a particular company—in Brome's case explicitly set out in a contract—none seem to have been sharers. Shakespeare was not only the Chamberlain's Men's house dramatist, producing on average two plays a year for them until his retirement, but also a close participant in their developing business.

A Gentlemen's Income

Either on the grounds of his reputation as a playwright alone or by virtue of a payment, Shakespeare had acquired a share in the new company and received his share of their fluctuating but sizeable profits over the rest of his life. The share also altered as the number of sharers varied, going from one-tenth in 1599 up to one-eighth when Will Kemp left and down to a twelfth and a fourteenth as further sharers were brought in. If the share was bought it was a shrewd investment, giving Shakespeare a certain amount of security of income, but it also conferred status on him as, in effect, a partner in a profit-sharing collective enterprise. . . .

Shakespeare and the Crown

The accession of James I brought the Chamberlain's Men an extraordinary honour: soon after arriving in London, James took over the company, now to be known as the King's Men. For the king's entry into London in May 1604, Shakespeare and the other players, like the members of the Queen's Men, Prince Henry's Men, and many other members of the royal household, were each given four and a half yards of red cloth, possibly to march in the procession or line the route. The King's Men frequently performed at the new court: between November 1604 and October 1605 they played eleven different works, seven of which were by Shakespeare, including new plays such as *Measure for Measure* and *Othello* and older ones such as *The Merchant of Venice* (twice) and *The Merry Wives of Windsor*, between the patent of May 1603 and Shakespeare's death they performed at court on at least 107 occasions. . . .

Political and other contemporary events affected the plays. . . . Both [*King*] *Lear* and *Macbeth* reflect in some ways the accession of King James: James's concern to unite Scotland and England seems to underpin the division of the kingdom in *Lear*, a warning of the consequences of disunity, while his claim of descent from Banquo is explicitly imaged in *Macbeth* where the witches show Macbeth the line of Banquo's descendants stretching towards James himself. *King Lear* also reflects a recent case in 1603 when Brian Annesley's eldest daughter tried to have her father declared insane and was prevented by the loving care of Annesley's youngest daughter, Cordell.

Yet if all these plays cannot be seen as other than tragedies, they are deliberately 'impure'. As Anthony Scoloker commented in 1604 in the epistle to his poem *Diaphantus*: a good poem should be 'like *Friendly Shakespeare's Tragedies*, where the *Commedian* rides, when the *Tragedian* stands on Tip-toe: Faith it should please all, like Prince *Hamlet*'. *Lear* and *Macbeth* are both based on events that, for Shakespeare and his audiences, were the stuff of the chronicles: for both, the source material lay in [the historical chronicles written by Raphael] Holinshed; both are histories, as the first published edition of *Lear* (1608) is identified on its title-page. . . .

The King's Men remained successful: at the celebrations for the marriage of James I's daughter to the elector palatine in February 1613 they performed fourteen plays, four of which were by Shakespeare.

The Gunpowder Plot and *Macbeth*

Peter Ackroyd

Peter Ackroyd, a Londoner, is a writer of best-selling and award-winning fiction and nonfiction. His books include Chaucer *and* London: The Biography.

In writing of the years 1605 and 1606 in Shakespeare's life, covering the writing and first productions of Macbeth, *Peter Ackroyd refers to Shakespeare's retirement from the stage and his investments made with the intent of setting himself up with a comfortable income and position in Stratford and providing for his family. In 1605 a group of pro-Catholic renegades, led by Robert Catesby, conspired to blow up the Protestant king, James I, and Parliament in what would become known as the Gunpowder Plot. After the conspirators' arrests, the government began a systematic persecution of Catholics. By July 1606, Ackroyd explains, Shakespeare had readied* Macbeth *for the stage, a play about a man who overthrows a king by murdering him and ordering further murders to retain his position. With its villainous usurper, the mention of King James's ancestor Banquo, and the evil Scottish witches like those who had earlier conspired against James,* Macbeth, *Ackroyd asserts, appears designed to please the king.*

On 24 July, 1605, Shakespeare invested £440 in tithes or, as the official document states, "one half of all tythes of corne and grayne aryseing within the townes, villages and fieldes of Old Stratford, Byshopton and Welcombe" as well as "half of all tythes of wooll and lambe, and of all small and privy tythes." A tithe had originally been a tenth part of the produce from the land, paid by farmer or tenant to the Church; this archaic form of tribute had then been passed to the Stratford Corporation at the time of the Reformation. Shakespeare was leasing his tithes from the corporation for a period of thirty-one years. At this late date it sounds a complicated matter, but at the time it was a conventional and familiar way of securing a reasonable income. The sum laid out by Shakespeare was in fact a very large one, and he could not raise the whole amount at one time; a year later he still owed some £20 to the vendor, Ralph Hubaud. He expected an annual return on his investment of something like £60, which was in itself a reasonable income. There were, however, one or two additional costs. He collected the tithes but was obligated to pay an annual fee of £17 to the Corporation of Stratford for the privilege. Nevertheless he still gathered a large amount.

The fact that his tithe lease ran for thirty-one years is evidence that he was intent upon securing his family's future after his death. It was a question of social, as well as financial, status. As the owner of tithes he was classified as a "lay rector," and had earned the right to be buried within the rails of the chancel of Stratford Church; it was a right that was taken up at his behest or on his behalf. Meanwhile his purchase of New Place had given him the right to a reserved pew in the church. He seems always to have been concerned about his precise social standing in his old town. It was in this period, too, that he rented out the eastern part of the family house in Henley Street to brewers by the name of Hiccox.

The transaction concerning the tithes was witnessed by two friends who would at a later date be named in his will, Anthony Nash of Welcombe and the lawyer Francis Collins. It is a mark of the invisibility of Shakespeare's Stratford life that little is known of these gentlemen, who played an intimate and familiar part in the dramatist's commercial affairs. They were part of a world very different from that of the players and playgoers, but he was equally at home in their company.

His prosperity did not go unremarked and in a fictional "biography" published [in] this year of a notorious highwayman, Gamaliel Ratsey, there are references to actors who "are grown so wealthy that they have expected to be knighted, or at least to be cojunct in authority and to sit with men of great worship." There is also a clear allusion to Shakespeare in the remark that "thou shalt learn to be *frugall* . . . to make thy hand a stranger to thy pocket . . . and when thou feelest thy purse well-lined, buy thee some *Place* or lordship in the country, that growing weary of playing thy mony may there bring thee to dignitie and reputation." The anonymous writer goes on to say that "I haue heard indeede, of some that haue gone to London very meanly, and haue come in time to be exceedingly wealthy." This fits Shakespeare's case exactly. The little volume seems to have been written by someone who knew of Shakespeare's affairs, and it is interesting that he should emphasise the dramatist's obvious thrift as well as his success.

The wealthy player is described as "weary of playing," too, which confirms the evidence that Shakespeare had retired from the stage by 1603 or 1604. The purchase of tithes, as we have seen, ensured that he had an annual and independent income larger than that of a player. It is doubly unlikely, then, that he was on tour with the King's Men in autumn and winter of this year. They were travelling again out of necessity, since a new onset of the plague meant that the theatres were closed from the middle of October to the middle of December. Among the plays they took with them were *Othello* and *Measure for Measure* as well as Ben Jonson's *Volpone*. They seem to have travelled as far west as Barnstaple, taking in Oxford and Saffron Walden en route, and may indeed have stayed in the provinces until the Globe was reopened on 15 December. Just eleven days later, they performed before the king.

Gunpowder Plot Conspirators. Public Domain.

They were playing in uncertain times, and to a king who was reported to be in a state of alarm and anxiety. In early November the conspiracy popularly known as the "Gunpowder Plot" was revealed to the world, with its ambitious and unprecedented attempt to blow up king and Parliament. It led to renewed suspicion and persecution of Roman Catholics, of course, nowhere more fiercely than in Stratford and [its county,] Warwickshire. The leading conspirator, Robert Catesby, was a Warwickshire man. The conspirators met in that county, and one of them had even rented Clopton House just outside Stratford to be close to his colleagues. In the immediate aftermath of the discovery of 5 November the bailiff of Stratford seized a cloak-bag "full of copes, vestments, crosses, crucifixes, chalices and other massing relics." It was supposed "to be delivered to one George Badger there." George Badger was the woollen-draper who lived next door to the Shakespeares in Henley Street. Shakespeare knew him very well indeed, and would have quickly been informed by his family of the calamity that had fallen upon him.

New legislation was passed by the Parliament against Catholic recusants, and the king himself, according to the Venetian ambassador, declared: "I shall most certainly be obliged to stain my hands with their blood, though sorely against my will . . ." For the Shakespeare family in Stratford, it was an uncertain time. In the spring of the following year, Susannah Shakespeare was cited for her failure to receive holy communion that Easter. She is listed with some well-known Catholic recusants in the town, among them Shakespeare's old friend Hamnet Sadler—the godfather of his dead son. The danger of her position must have been emphasised to her by someone close to her, since the word "*dismissa*" [dismissed] was later placed against her entry. She must have outwardly conformed by taking communion. Three years later, however, Richard Shakespeare, the dramatist's brother, was taken before the bawdry court at Stratford for some unspecified offence; he was fined 12 pence, for the use of the Stratford poor, which suggests that he was found guilty of breaking the Sabbath.

The response of Shakespeare to the turbulent events of 1605 was to write a play of apparently conservative and orthodox intent. *Macbeth* was concerned with the terrible consequences of murdering a divinely appointed sovereign, and within the drama itself there are even references to the trials of the conspirators in the spring of 1606. There are allusions to "equivocation," a concept which appeared at the trial of the Jesuit Father Henry Garnet, who was subsequently hanged. When Lady Macduff remarks, on the subject of treason, "every one that do's so, is a Traitor, and must be hang'd" (1512) there may have been applause and cheers among the audience of the Globe. In *Macbeth*, too, there is an invocation of the Stuart dynasty, with reference to the kings who will rule England as well as Scotland. Since the play is also steeped in King James's favourite subject, witchcraft, there can be no doubt that it was purposefully designed to appeal to the new monarch. The witches of *Macbeth* can be said to plot against the lawful king, with their intimations of Macbeth's greatness, and just fifteen years previously some Scottish witches had been tried for conspiring against James himself. The parallel is clear. In the previous year, too, King James had been greeted by three sibyls at the gates of an Oxford college and hailed as the true descendant of Banquo. That is no doubt why Shakespeare, in direct contrast with the source, refuses to connect Banquo with the Macbeths' plot against Duncan. Shakespeare was adapting James's own suppositions and beliefs into memorable theatre. He was in a sense sanctifying them and turning them into myth.

Yet Shakespeare wrote with only one eye upon the king. *Macbeth* was also designed to entertain everyone else. It ushers on to the stage ghosts as well as bloodshed and magic. What could be more appealing to an early seventeenth-century audience than royalty and mystery combined? The scene at the banquet, in which Banquo's ghost appears to Macbeth, mightily impressed itself upon Shakespeare's contemporaries. It is a play that acquired an almost Celtic sense of doom and the supernatural. That is why actors refuse to name it *Macbeth*, but to this day continue to call it "the Scottish play." It is as if Shakespeare, deep in his Scottish sources, was possessed by a new form of imagination; it is a tribute to his extraordinary sensitivity and to his unconscious powers of assimilation.

Macbeth is one of the shortest plays that Shakespeare ever wrote—in fact only *The Comedy of Errors* is shorter—and has a playing time of approximately two hours. It is also remarkably free of oaths and profanities, as a result of a measure passed by Parliament in March 1603; a parliamentary act to "restrain the abuses of players" forbade irreverence or blasphemy on the public stage. It has been suggested that the relative brevity of the play is an indication of the king's span of attention, but this is unlikely. It may have been the result of cuts by the Master of the Revels. More likely, however, is that the play itself demanded this length. The intensity and concentration of the fatal action require a series of drumbeats. Although the slight ambiguity in the respective roles of Macbeth and Lady Macbeth suggests that Shakespeare may have begun the play without knowing which of them would kill the king, there is a consistency of effect. The verse is shaped and pared down so that it becomes echoic; it is almost relentless in its pace, and there are images throughout of rushing action. "Time" is mentioned on forty-four occasions. There are no puns, and only one "comic" scene in which the Porter responds to the knocking at the gate; it is hardly comic, however, since the Porter is modelled upon the keeper of Hell's gates and the elaborate references in the Porter's monologue to the details of the recent conspiracy are pervaded by a chilling gallow' humour.

The Porter is indeed an image of the Hell Porter in the mystery plays, and it has been well observed that the banqueting scene in the play is related to the scene of feasting in that part of the mystery cycle entitled "The Death of Herod." The death and doom of the ancient plays survive in Shakespeare's dramaturgy, as another layer of darkness and supernatural fear. Shakespeare is much more concerned with the ancient forces of the earth than with the omens of the sky. *Macbeth* is a poem of the night. Yet, in any discussion of Macbeth himself, the concept of darkness is not required. He is the most vital and energetic character within the play, a natural force, surpassing any conventional notion of good and evil. He partakes of the sublime. Like many of Shakespeare's tragic protagonists, he seems actively to seek out his fate.

Since the play is mentioned in a production by the Children of St. Paul's in early July 1606, it must have been performed at the Globe before that date. So *Macbeth* was played during the season that ran from Easter on 21 April until the middle of July, when once more the playhouses were closed as a result of the plague. The King's Men remained in the neighbourhood of London for a short period, however, in order to entertain King Christian of Denmark, who was the brother-in-law of James; he remained in England from 15 July to 11 August, and [Globe share owner John] Heminges was paid for "three playes before his Majestie and the kinge of Denmarke at Greenwich and Hampton Court." It has plausibly been asserted that one of these plays was *Macbeth*, performed before the royal parties in the early days of August.

After their royal performances the King's Men began a season of touring in Kent, where they played at Dover, Maidstone and Faversham. They also journeyed to Saffron Walden, Leicester, Oxford, and Marlborough. It is tempting to believe that Shakespeare was with them when they visited Dover, at the beginning of October, if only because of the important presence of that town in his next play. But such explicit connections are dangerous. There is no reason to suppose that Shakespeare travelled with them, and every reason to believe that he was engaged elsewhere. In the course of this year, after all, he completed the writing of *King Lear*.

Chapter 2

Macbeth and Power

Darkness in the Struggle for Power

A.C. Bradley

A.C. Bradley, an Oxford don and one of the earliest enduring analysts of Shakespeare, published his seminal work, Shakespearean Tragedy, *in 1904.*

In the following selection, A.C. Bradley explores atmosphere and character in Macbeth, *as well as questions of fate and personal choice in Macbeth's unbridled ambition, which he sees as the chief problem of the play. Images of blackness and night prevail in the play, highlighted by flashes of vivid color, suggesting blood and emphasizing guilt. Even nature attests to human guilt and malice, a matter shown by Shakespeare's ironic juxtaposition of people and events. The witches, while they add striking atmosphere, are often given too much credit for their role in Macbeth's pursuit of power. Macbeth's evil ambition, however, comes not from the witches, but from within himself. Although Macbeth is damned even after the first murder, Bradley contends that he still evokes sympathy in his inexorable doom because of his "native love of goodness" and his "tragic grandeur."*

Macbeth, it is probable, was the last-written of the four great tragedies. . . . In that play Shakespeare's final style appears for the first time completely formed, and the transition to this style is much more decidedly visible in *Macbeth* than in *King Lear*. Yet in certain respects *Macbeth* recalls *Hamlet* rather than *Othello* or *King Lear*. In the heroes of both plays the passage from thought to a critical resolution and action is difficult, and excites the keenest interest. In neither play, as in *Othello* and *King Lear*, is painful pathos one of the

A.C. Bradley, *Shakespearean Tragedy: Lectures on "Hamlet," "Othello," "King Lear," "Macbeth."* Basingstoke, Hampshire: Macmillan and Co., 1951. Pp. 331–65. Reproduced with permission of Palgrave Macmillan.

main effects. Evil, again, though it shows in *Macbeth* a prodigious energy, is not the icy or stony inhumanity of Iago [in *Othello*] or Goneril [in *King Lear*]; and, as in *Hamlet*, it is pursued by remorse. Finally, Shakespeare no longer restricts the action to purely human agencies, as in the two preceding tragedies; portents once more fill the heavens, ghosts rise from their graves, an unearthly light flickers about the head of the doomed man. The special popularity of *Hamlet* and *Macbeth* is due in part to some of these common characteristics, notably to the fascination of the supernatural, the absence of the spectacle of extreme undeserved suffering, the absence of characters which horrify and repel and yet are destitute of grandeur. . . .

Foreboding Darkness

Darkness, we may even say blackness, broods over this tragedy. It is remarkable that almost all the scenes which at once recur to memory take place either at night or in some dark spot. The vision of the dagger, the murder of Duncan, the murder of Banquo, the sleep-walking of Lady Macbeth, all come in night-scenes. The Witches dance in the thick air of a storm, or, 'black and midnight hags,' receive Macbeth in a cavern. The blackness of night is to the hero a thing of fear, even of horror; and that which he feels becomes the spirit of the play. The faint glimmerings of the western sky at twilight are here menacing: it is the hour when the traveller hastens to reach safety in his inn, and when Banquo rides homeward to meet his assassins; the hour when 'light thickens,' when 'night's black agents to their prey do rouse,' when the wolf begins to howl, and the owl to scream, and withered murder steals forth to his work. Macbeth bids the stars hide their fires that his 'black' desires may be concealed; Lady Macbeth calls on thick night to come, palled in the dunnest smoke of hell. . . .

Images of Blood

The atmosphere of *Macbeth*, however, is not that of unrelieved blackness. On the contrary, as compared with *King Lear* and its cold dim gloom, *Macbeth* leaves a decided impression of colour; it is really the impression of a black night broken by flashes of light and colour, sometimes vivid and even glaring. They are the lights and colours of the thunder-storm in the first scene; of the dagger hanging before Macbeth's eyes and glittering alone in the midnight air; of the torch borne by the servant when he and his lord come upon Banquo crossing the castle-court to his room; of the torch, again, which Fleance carried to light his father to death, and which was dashed out by one of the murderers; of the torches that flared in the hall on the face of the Ghost and the blanched cheeks of Macbeth; of the flames beneath the boiling caldron from which the apparitions in the cavern rose; of the taper which showed to the Doctor and Gentlewoman the wasted face and blank eyes of Lady Macbeth. And, above all, the colour is the colour of blood. . . . What pictures are those of the murderer appearing at the door of the banquet-room with Banquo's 'blood upon his face'; of Banquo himself 'with twenty trenched gashes on his head,' or 'bloodbolter'd' and smiling in derision at his murderer; of Macbeth, gazing at his hand, and watching it dye the whole green ocean red; of Lady Macbeth, gazing at hers, and stretching it away from her face to escape the smell of blood that all the perfumes of Arabia will not subdue! The most horrible lines in the whole tragedy are those of her shuddering cry, 'Yet who would have thought the old man to have had so much blood in him?' And it is not only at such moments that these images occur. Even in the quiet conversation of Malcolm and Macduff, Macbeth is imagined as holding a bloody sceptre, and Scotland as a country bleeding and receiving every day a new gash added to her wounds. . . .

The Witches and Macbeth's Choice

On the one hand the Witches, whose contribution to the 'atmosphere' of *Macbeth* can hardly be exaggerated, are credited with far too great an influence upon the action; sometimes they are described as goddesses, or even as fates, whom Macbeth is powerless to resist. And this is perversion. On the other hand, we are told that, great as is their influence on the action, it is so because they are merely symbolic representations of the unconscious or half-conscious guilt in Macbeth himself. And this is inadequate.

The Witches . . . are not goddesses, or fates, or, in any way whatever, supernatural beings. They are old women, poor and ragged, skinny and hideous, full of vulgar spite, occupied in killing their neighbours' swine or revenging themselves on sailors' wives who have refused them chestnuts. . . .

Macbeth himself nowhere betrays a suspicion that his action is, or has been, thrust on him by an external power. He curses the Witches for deceiving him, but he never attempts to shift to them the burden of his guilt. Neither has Shakespeare placed in the mouth of any other character in this play such fatalistic expressions as may be found in *King Lear* and occasionally elsewhere. He appears actually to have taken pains to make the natural psychological genesis of Macbeth's crimes perfectly clear. . . .

The Witches and their prophecies, it they are to be rationalised or taken symbolically, must represent not only the evil slumbering in the hero's soul, but all those obscurer influences of the evil around him in the world which aid his own ambition and the incitements of his wife. Such influences, even if we put aside all belief in evil 'spirits,' are as certain, momentous, and terrifying facts as the presence of inchoate evil in the soul itself; and if we exclude all reference to these facts from our idea of the Witches, it will be greatly impoverished and will certainly fail to correspond with the imaginative effect. . . .

The words of the Witches are fatal to the hero only because there is in him something which leaps into light at the sound of them; but they are at the same time the witness of forces which never cease to work in the world around him, and, on the instant of his surrender to them, entangle him inextricably in the web of Fate. . . .

The "Passion of Ambition"

From this murky background stand out the two great terrible figures, who dwarf all the remaining characters of the drama. Both are sublime, and both inspire, far more than the other tragic heroes, the feeling of awe. They are never detached in imagination from the atmosphere which surrounds them and adds to their grandeur and terror. It is, as it were, continued into their souls. For within them is all that we felt without—the darkness of night, lit with the flame of tempest and the hues of blood, and haunted by wild and direful shapes, 'murdering ministers,' spirits of remorse, and maddening visions of peace lost and judgment to come. The way to be untrue to Shakespeare here, as always, is to relax the tension of imagination, to conventionalise, to conceive Macbeth, for example, as a half-hearted cowardly criminal, and Lady Macbeth as a whole-hearted fiend.

These two characters are fired by one and the same passion of ambition and to a considerable extent they are alike. . . .

The Complexity of Macbeth's Character

Macbeth, the cousin of a King mild, just, and beloved, but now too old to lead his army, is introduced to us as a general, of extraordinary prowess, who has covered himself with glory in putting down a rebellion and repelling the invasion of a foreign army. In these conflicts he showed great personal courage, a quality which he continues to display throughout the drama in regard to all plain dangers. It is difficult to be sure of his customary demeanour, for in the play we see him either in what appears to be an exceptional relation to his wife, or else in the throes of remorse and desperation; but from his behaviour during his journey home after the war, from his *later* conversations with Lady Macbeth, and from his language to the murderers of Banquo and to others, we imagine him as a great warrior, somewhat masterful, rough, and abrupt, a man to inspire some fear and much admiration. . . .

At the same time he was exceedingly ambitious. He must have been so by temper. The tendency must have been greatly strengthened by his marriage. When we see him, it has been further stimulated by his remarkable success and by the consciousness of exceptional powers and merit. It becomes a passion. The course of action suggested by it is extremely perilous: it sets his good name, his position, and even his life on the hazard. It is also abhorrent to his better feelings. Their defeat in the struggle with ambition leaves him utterly wretched, and would have kept him so, however complete had been his outward success and security. On the other hand, his passion for power and his instinct of self-assertion are so vehement that no inward misery could persuade him to relinquish the fruits of crime, or to advance from remorse to repentance. . . .

Macbeth's better nature—to put the matter for clearness' sake too broadly—instead of speaking to him in the overt language of moral ideas, commands, and prohibitions, incorporates itself in images which alarm and horrify. His imagination is thus the best of him; something usually deeper and higher than his conscious thoughts; and if he had obeyed it he would have been safe. But his wife quite misunderstands it, and he himself understands it only in part. The terrifying images which deter him from crime and follow its commission, and which are really the protest of his deepest self, seem to his wife the creations of mere nervous fear, and are sometimes referred by himself to the dread of vengeance or the restlessness of insecurity. His conscious or reflective mind, that is, moves chiefly among considerations of outward success and failure, while his inner being is convulsed by conscience. And his inability to understand himself is repeated and exaggerated in the interpretations of actors and critics, who represent him as a coward, cold-blooded, calculating, and pitiless, who shrinks from crime simply because it is dangerous, and suffers afterwards simply because he is not safe. In reality his courage is frightful. He strides from crime to crime, though his soul never ceases to bar his advance with shapes of terror, or to clamour in his ears that he is murdering his peace and casting away his 'eternal jewel.' . . .

No Repentance

What appalls him is always the image of his own guilty heart or bloody deed, or some image which derives from them its terror or gloom. These, when they arise, hold him spell-bound and possess him wholly, like a hypnotic trance which is at the same time the ecstasy of a poet. As the first 'horrid image' of Duncan's murder—of himself murdering Duncan—rises from unconsciousness and confronts him, his hair stands on end and the outward scene vanishes from his eyes. Why? For fear of 'consequences'? The idea is ridiculous. Or because the deed is bloody? The man who with his 'smoking' steel 'carved out his passage' to the rebel leader, and 'unseam'd him from the nave to the chaps,' would hardly be frightened by blood. How could fear of consequences make the dagger he is to use hang suddenly glittering before him in the air, and then as suddenly dash it with gouts of blood? Even when he *talks* of consequences, and declares that if he were safe against them he would 'jump the life to come,' his imagination bears witness against him, and shows us that what really holds him back is the hideous vileness of the deed:

> He's here in double trust;
> First, as I am his kinsman and his subject,
> Strong both against the deed; then, as his host,
> Who should against his murderer shut the door,

> Not bear the knife myself. Besides, this Duncan
> Hath borne his faculties so meek, hath been
> So clear in his great office, that his virtues
> Will plead like angels, trumpet-tongued, against
> The deep damnation of his taking-off;
> And pity, like a naked new-born babe,
> Striding the blast, or heaven's cherubim, horsed
> Upon the sightless couriers of the air,
> Shall blow the horrid deed in every eye,
> That tears shall drown the wind.

It may be said that he is here thinking of the horror that others will feel at the deed—thinking therefore of consequences. Yes, but could he realise thus how horrible the deed would look to others if it were not equally horrible to himself? . . .

But he has never, to put it pedantically, accepted as the principle of his conduct the morality which takes shape in his imaginative fears. Had he done so, and said plainly to his wife, 'The thing is vile, and, however much I have sworn to do it, I will not,' she would have been helpless; for all her arguments proceed on the assumption that there is for them no such point of view. Macbeth does approach this position once, when, resenting the accusation of cowardice, he answers,

I dare do all that may become a
man;
Who dares do more is none.

She feels in an instant that everything is at stake, and, ignoring the point, overwhelms him with indignant and contemptuous personal reproach. But he yields to it because he is himself half-ashamed of that answer of his, and because, for want of habit, the simple idea which it expresses has, no hold on him comparable to the force it acquires when it becomes incarnate in visionary fears and warnings.

Yet these were so insistent, and they offered to his ambition a resistance so strong, that it is impossible to regard him as falling through the blindness or delusion of passion. On the contrary, he himself feels with such intensity the enormity of his purpose that, it seems clear, neither his ambition nor yet the prophecy of the Witches would ever without the aid of Lady Macbeth have overcome this feeling. As it is, the deed is done in horror and without the faintest desire or sense of glory—done, one may almost say, as if it were an appalling duty; and, the instant it is finished, its futility is revealed to Macbeth as clearly as its vileness had been revealed beforehand. As he staggers from the scene he mutters in despair,

Wake Duncan with thy knocking! I
would thou could'st.

The Love of Power

That heart-sickness which comes from Macbeth's perception of the futility of his crime, and which never leaves him for long, is not, however, his habitual state. It could not be so, for two reasons. In the first place the consciousness of guilt is stronger in him than the consciousness of failure; and it keeps him in a perpetual agony of restlessness, and forbids him simply to droop and pine. His mind is 'full of scorpions.' He cannot sleep. He 'keeps alone,' moody and savage. 'All that is within him does condemn itself for being there.' There is a fever in his blood which urges him to ceaseless action in the search for oblivion. And, in the second place, ambition, the love of power, the instinct of self-assertion, are much too potent in Macbeth to permit him to resign, even in spirit, the prize for which he has put rancours in the vessel of his peace. The 'will to live' is mighty in him. The forces which impelled him to aim at the crown re-assert themselves. He faces the world, and his own conscience, desperate, but never dreaming of acknowledging defeat. He will see 'the frame of things disjoint' first. He challenges fate into the lists. . . .

In the very depths a gleam of his native love of goodness, and with it a touch of tragic grandeur, rests upon him. The evil he has desperately embraced continues to madden or to wither his inmost heart. No experience in the world could bring him to glory in it or make his peace with it, or to forget what he once was.

Shifting Values, Chaos, and Order in *Macbeth*

Terence Hawkes

Terence Hawkes, senior lecturer emeritus in English at University College, Cardiff, is the author of Shakespeare and the Reason *and* Shakespeare's Talking Animals. *He is also editor of the* Accents on Shakespeare *editions.*

In the context of England's defeat of the Spanish Armada in 1588, as well as the upheaval that followed the demise of King Henry VIII, old values and systems based on an acceptance of monarchs as divine arbiters were threatened by vain usurpations of power. This shift is shown dramatically by Shakespeare in Macbeth's final descent into oblivion. In the following selection, Terence Hawkes discusses the explosive new order, which attacks the monarchy and the old order. He discusses the violence, the Gunpowder Plot of 1605, the rule of James I, and Shakespeare's flattery of the new king in his identification of James with good King Duncan. Despite its historical setting, the meaning of the play for audiences transcends times and customs.

Macbeth has increasingly impressed twentieth century critics as a play with a peculiarly modern bearing. Despite its evident involvement with an older world, with witches, their incantations and their spells, those who have written about the play in our own time indicate a growing sense that its protagonist speaks with a modern voice, from within a modern political and moral situation, about modern matters. . . .

We might begin to account for this phenomenon by means of the large, confirming observation that the play's date and

Terence Hawkes, Introduction to *Twentieth Century Interpretations of "Macbeth."* Upper Saddle River, NJ: Prentice-Hall, 1977. Pp. 1–12.

place of composition, London 1605 to 1606, seem in general terms to locate it at the beginning of that vast and complex process of economic, religious, and political development in Western Europe from which the modern world was to emerge. Much of *Macbeth*'s hold on us possibly derives from the oblique but penetrative insights it offers into the nature of that world as judged by the standards of an older, yet still living medieval one. And so, when Macbeth complains

> I have lived long enough. My way of life
>
> Is fall'n into the sear, the yellow leaf,
>
> And that which should accompany old age,
>
> As honour, love, obedience, troops of friends,
>
> I must not look to have; but in their stead,
>
> Curses not loud but deep, mouth-honour, breath,
>
> Which the poor heart would fain deny, and dare not.
>
> (V. iii. 22–28)

The general diagnosis this implies of the new world at its commencement perhaps seems peculiarly apt to those who now sense its conclusion. *Macbeth* witnesses a birth: we are in at the death.

But maybe we can also be more specific. On 5 November 1605 a search by security forces, instituted at the personal behest of King James, discovered beneath the Houses of Parliament a secret cache containing enough gunpowder, fuses, and other implements to blow the king, his ministers, and the lawful government of the entire state sky-high.

It would be difficult to overestimate the shock this discovery generated amongst the population at large. The whole affair instantly found itself raised to the level of trauma by the propaganda rapidly instigated by James and his advisers and it quickly acquired dimensions resonant far beyond the immediate facts at issue. The event is celebrated in Britain to this day with bonfires, fireworks, and the burning in effigy of one of the conspirators. It was as if a new destructive, reductive age had begun—its dawn the light of the terrorist's match.

Glynne Wickham has recently drawn attention to the extent of the implications derived at the time from the Gunpowder Plot and its discovery: in particular, to the larger symbolic role James' own writings and speeches carefully gave it. It would of course be mistaken to argue that *Macbeth* in any sense takes the Plot as its direct subject: the relationship of great art to reality is rarely of that overt order. But it is not surprising that a play dealing explicitly with James' personal ancestry should contain at its core precise references to the trial of one of the alleged conspirators (in the Porter scene) or that the wider social, spiritual, and theological ramifications of the Plot—fully exploited by James in his pronouncements on the subject—should find themselves obliquely embodied in a play whose first performance (the evidence suggests) took place at Hampton Court in his presence and that of his guest, King Christian IV of Denmark.

In essence, the Plot's intent was, almost literally, shattering. Following Queen Elizabeth's death in 1603, James' accession to the throne in the same year had seemed to offer a solution to many of the problems facing England both at home and abroad. Moreover, it had seemed to hold out a specific promise in a particular case. James was already King James VI of Scotland. His presence on the throne of England seemed to presage the final, peaceful union of those two nations. As

King James I of England. Getty Images. Reproduced by permission.

James VI and I in one person, he seemed to represent and literally to embody peaceful unity: that final knitting together of the peoples of England, Scotland, and Wales into a political and cultural identity whose imperial destiny was God-given and manifest, and for which the name "Great Britain" had recently been devised. The reunification of Britain, and the reunification of religion within Britain, stood as major items in the "scenario" of his reign that had been officially propagated. James was to be the second Brutus, destined to reunify the land founded by the first Brutus, and then riven by him in his folly. And it was that edifice of imminent unity that the Gunpowder Plot seemed designed to reduce to rubble. That the conspirators were foreign-backed Catholics, their confessions appeared to confirm. That they were also (and therefore) agents of the devil intent upon the destruction of God's divine plan for Great Britain and her people followed without question. Inspired by Lucifer, the conflagration they purposed had its analogue in the flames of Hell.

One of the central concerns of *Macbeth* is of course the disunity and disorder that the murder of King Duncan brings to Scotland. . . .

At its most fundamental level, the murder of Duncan results in the overthrow of a social structure based on principles of one sort, and its replacement by another structure based on principles of an opposite sort. Macbeth's crime violates, as he recognizes, the traditional "double trust" of loyalty and hospitality. He should

> against his murderer shut the door
>
> Not bear the knife myself.
>
> (I. vii. 15–16)

After that violation, and because of it, the traditionally ordered society in which the guarantee of each man's position (even Macbeth's) resides in the monarch's own supremacy is replaced by a society in which the only guarantee seems to reside in the exercise of brute force. . . .

The model for such reduction presents itself right at the beginning of the play in the language of those sources of evil whose influence on Macbeth proves so dire. In its deliberate obfuscation, its ambiguity, its concern to mislead rather than inform, the language of the Witches demands that we judge it to be deliberately and fundamentally subversive. It seeks to overturn that ordering of the world which every society makes and, perceiving its own version as "natural," takes as the basis of normality. "Fair is foul and foul is fair" aptly represents its principal objective: the reversal of accepted values. . . .

. . . In fact, with unity finally rehabilitated, the new king safely *en route* to his coronation, and James' ancestors amply restored thereby to the status which he, currently a member of the audience, inherits and embodies, the play's own "poor players" may be said to have been involved in concrete matters of some moment, with a continuity far outlasting their "hour upon the stage." As a result, *Macbeth* concludes by paying the living monarch a fine dramatic compliment.

But of course this constitutes only the climax of that series of insistent, oblique references to James which runs throughout *Macbeth* and marks one of its most distinctive features. The English king's healing touch described in Act IV, and said there to be passed on "to the succeeding royalty" (IV, iii, 155), unmistakably acknowledges James' own recent revival of the practice of "touching" for the King's Evil (scrofula); his continuing interest in witches meets an obvious response in a play that also confirms his own judgment, made in a learned study, *Daemonologie* (1597), that they were agents of the devil. By such glancing allusions, as well as others mentioned above, *Macbeth* ultimately seems almost to reach out and embrace the king in its action. As it does so, it may be said to redeem, by the vitality of that relationship with the living world, the sterile, reduced, and dead world of its protagonist. And the king and his royal guests, who began the performance as spectators, thus end it as participants. . . .

Of course, *Macbeth* is a tragedy and its implications reach far beyond the simple optimism that the compliment to James appears to suggest. Most modern critics agree that the play exhibits more concern with the diagnosis of evil in the modern world than with flattery of its royal audience. We may miss the purely "local" allusions, but Macbeth's reduced world, its language, its politics, are instantly familiar to us. . . .

The Clash Between Military and Christian Virtues

Jan H. Blits

Jan H. Blits, professor of philosophy and literature at the University of Delaware, has authored The End of the Ancient Republic: Shakespeare's "Julius Caesar" *and* The Insufficiency of Virtue: "Macbeth" and the Natural Order, *from which the following viewpoint is taken.*

In this selection, Jan H. Blits sees Macbeth *as positing a medieval Christian cosmos in which God is omnipotent, guarding and guiding the world through a natural, hierarchical order, of which human morality is a part. Major characters, including the Macbeths, the Macduffs, and the Old Man, accept this divine order. Blits asserts that tension exists, however, between two kinds of accepted virtue: one representing manly or military actions, the other Christian gentleness. Thus Macbeth, a Christian warrior responding to the manly or military side of this dual ethic, is goaded into action by his wife's charge of weakness. But his conscience destroys him. He violates the moral order and the source of life. Ultimately possessing a "fruitless" crown, he stands for death, not life, in contrast to Lady Macduff who represents womanly, Christian virtue.*

Macbeth depicts the life and soul of a Christian warrior who first becomes his kingdom's savior, then its criminal king, and finally its bloody tyrant. Set in eleventh-century Scotland, the play portrays Macbeth within the context of a moral and political order rooted in a natural order that is established by God. Far from being merely a backdrop for the play (as is often suggested), this natural order decisively shapes

Jan H. Blits, Introduction to *The Insufficiency of Virtue: "Macbeth" and the Natural Order*. Lanham, MD: Rowman & Littlefield, 1996. Pp. 1–7.

both the characters and the action of the drama. Shakespeare shows that what a character thinks about the natural order affects how he understands the moral and political world, and hence himself and his life. It makes him who or what he is.

The natural order that we see in *Macbeth* is a distinctly medieval Christian cosmos. Characterized by God's providence, plentitude, and pervasive presence, it appears to be a hierarchical, harmonious unity in which all being and goodness flow from God and what everything in the world is depends on God and its place in his scheme of creation. Throughout the play, something's "place" is not merely its spatial location, but its fixed "degree" or "rank" in the established order of things. Place refers to hierarchical position as well as to whereabouts in space. Likewise, God is generally thought not only to see everyone's every action and to know everyone's most secret thoughts ("Heaven knows what she has known" [5.1.46]), but to protect the innocent, punish the guilty, and, indeed, to feed the birds of the air and supply their other natural needs. Nothing escapes Heaven's notice or concern. Even Macbeth and Lady Macbeth fear that Heaven will see them murdering Duncan and act to stop or to avenge the deed. . . .

Power and the Complexity of Virtue

Since God wills and orders all things and nothing happens outside his providence, many of the characters in *Macbeth* believe that chance or fortune has little or no role in human affairs. Not only does the traditionally pious Old Man trust that good always comes of evil (2.4.40–41), but Macbeth and Lady Macbeth, on the one side, and Macduff and Lady Macduff, on the other, show by their actions as well as by their words that they believe that virtue possesses the power to govern the world. Notwithstanding their deep and direct moral opposition in other critical respects, each of them sees the world as a morally consistent order in which the virtuous are always rewarded or protected and virtue alone determines one's fate.

Shakespeare leads us, however, to examine the unity, harmony, and order of this medieval Christian cosmos. The medieval world—imbued with distinct and fixed ranks, the subordination and obedience of the lower to the higher, and a strong sense of plentitude, purpose, wholeness, and order in both the temporal and the spiritual realms—may set forth the natural order in high relief. But, in so doing, it also points up fundamental tensions that inhere not only within the medieval cosmos, but, by implication, within any unified, harmonious, natural order. In *Macbeth* we see two such tensions. One concerns the relation between two opposed-forms of virtue; the other, the relation between virtue and life. The tensions themselves and the complex interaction between them, played out in the actions and the souls of the characters, form the essential core of the drama.

Saintly Virtue and Manly Power

The first tension exists between the two contrasting forms of virtue esteemed in *Macbeth*'s warrior, Christian Scotland: the manly virtue practiced by men like Macbeth ("brave Macbeth (well he deserves that name)" [1.2.16]) and honored so highly by his wife, and the Christian virtue evoked by the "most sainted king" Duncan (4.3.109) and devoutly revered by Macduff. Manly virtue honors bravery, boldness, and resolution ("Be bloody, bold, and resolute" [4.1.79]); Christian virtue exalts meekness, innocence, and trust ("Whither should I fly? / I have done no harm" [4.2.72–73]). The former emphasizes fear while honoring war; the latter emphasizes love while celebrating peace. Manly virtue speaks of courage, action, prowess, vengeance, and resistance. It demands action while disdaining fortune. Christian virtue speaks of pity, patience, guilt, forgiveness, and remorse. It demands innocence while trusting providence. What is fair in the light of one is foul in the light of the other.

In *Macbeth*, Christian and warrior virtue exist side by side not only in the same country, but often in the same individual. While Macbeth, for example, . . . is spurred to Duncan's murder by his wife's accusation of unmanliness ("When you durst do it, then you were a man" [1.7.49]), he nonetheless not only looks up to Duncan's meek, angel-like virtues, but, repulsed by his thoughts of murder and eventually tormented by his murderous deeds, he is finally destroyed by his own Christian conscience. Indeed, haunted by his guilty conscience, he tries to destroy it and, in so doing, ultimately destroys both his conscience and himself. If manly ambition leads Macbeth to his first crime, paradoxically it is Christian conscience that drives him to his last. Had he either listened to his Christian conscience in the beginning or never heard it at all, he would not have become a bloody tyrant in the end.

The most obvious example of these oppos'd virtues coexisting in the same person, each in an untempered form, is Macduff. Macduff is at once a manly warrior and a devout Christian. No one, not even Macbeth, speaks more often or more assuredly of his sword than he ("My voice is in my sword" [5.8.7]) Nor does anyone else, not even the pious Old Man in act 2, scene 4, describe Scotland's moral and political events in explicitly biblical, let alone apocalyptical, terms so frequently or so emphatically as Macduff, repeatedly, does. Macduff trusts his sword and the cross equally. Thus he flees to England to bring back an army to overthrow Macbeth ("Let us rather / Hold fast the mortal sword, and like good men / Bestride our downfall'n birthdom" [4.3.2–4]). But, while doing so, he leaves his wife and children undefended, trusting their protection to God. And then, upon hearing of their slaughter, he does not doubt divine providence, but blames his own sinfulness for their fate:

Did Heaven look on,

And would not take their part?
Sinful Macduff!

They were all struck for thee.
Naught that I am,

Not for their own demerits, but for
mine,

Fell slaughter on their souls.

(4.3.223–27)

Even while he believes that only the mortal sword can redeem Scotland's great wrongs, Macduff also believes in the existence of a moral order in which God guarantees the victory of goodness in the world and allows only sinners (or those they love) to suffer.

Similarly, Duncan, though completely lacking martial virtue, takes enormous delight in the bloody Captain's grisly account of the brave Macbeth. Disdaining fortune with his brandished sword, Macbeth carved his way through the rebels until he came face to face with their leader, whom he immediately ripped open from his navel to his jaw and whose head he then fixed upon the battlements. "O valiant cousin! worthy gentleman!" (1.2.24), the "most sainted king" exclaims. And the bloody Captain himself, epitomizing the confusion, declares that he "cannot tell" whether Macbeth and Banquo "meant to bathe in reeking wounds, / Or memorize another Golgotha" (1.2.42, 40–41). To this good and hardy Scottish soldier, a warrior's bloodbath seems indistinguishable from the Crucifixion. . . .

Violation of the Order of Nature

Nature is associated throughout *Macbeth* with two things; with order and with life. The moral order is seen as part of the natural order, and the natural order is the source of, sustains, and, indeed, is characterized by, life. While in our day the prevailing view is that nature is essentially inanimate (inert matter in aimless motion) and freedom from nature, or even opposition to it, is the source of morality, in Macbeth's medieval Scotland, just the opposite seems the case. Nature is seen as embracing and sustaining both virtue and life. The source of the one, it is also the source of the other. It holds the moral and the biological realms together.

Thus, nature is often associated in *Macbeth* with gentleness ("the milk of human kindness" [1.5.17]), with pity and remorse ("the compunctious visitings of Nature" [1.5.45]), with nourishment ("great Nature's second course" [2.2.38]), with bountiful giving ("the gift [of] . . . bounteous Nature" [3.1.97]), and with a parent's love ("the natural touch" [4.2.9]). Its opposite is not so much convention or even the supernatural, both of which abound in *Macbeth*, as it is death or murder. "Death and Nature do contend about them," says Lady Macbeth, "Whether they live, or die" (2.2.7–8) . . .

Manliness and Motherliness

Lady Macbeth, the voice of manly, warrior virtue in its wholly untempered form (1.7.49–51), fears that her husband is too full of the milk of human kindness. She wishes to unsex herself—to have murdering spirits come to her breasts and take her milk for gall—so that she would be cruel enough to kill Duncan. Indeed, she would rather murder her own son than forswear her promise to murder the king. In direct contrast, Lady Macduff, the voice of womanly, Christian virtue in its untempered form (4.2.72–78), fears her husband's lack of human kindness. Identified by Shakespeare only as "wife" and "mother," she is all maternal love (4.2.8 ff.). She even refuses to hear that any other of Macduff's loves could possibly compete with his love as a husband and father. One woman wishes that both she and her husband were all manly; the other seems to be all womanly and wishes her husband were more so. Yet, even though these two women—the only women of major importance in the play apart from the Witches—represent opposite sides of the tension within virtue, both believe in the sovereign power of virtue. Just as Macduff thinks that only sinners suffer, his wife thinks that innocence suffices for safety.

The Course of Macbeth's Drive for Power

Paul Fletcher

Paul Fletcher is professor emeritus of English at Langside College, Glasgow, Scotland.

In the following selection, Paul Fletcher follows the course of Macbeth's overweaning ambition, with commentaries on his past as a warrior, his ambition being aroused by the witches, and his being taunted by his even more ambitious wife. Fletcher describes Lady Macbeth's part in the murder of Duncan and points out that one murder must inevitably lead to another in Macbeth's drive for the throne. In the end, Macbeth is punished for his murders committed in the name of kingly ambition.

A special feature of *Macbeth* is the presentation of evil as a force working through witches, creatures endowed with supernatural powers, and, just as evil human beings in Shakespeare characteristically employ deception to work their will on their victims, so too do the Witches—Macbeth, having been lured by them into evil, finds himself the victim of their deception.

The Bloody Warrior

At the beginning of the play Macbeth is a highly esteemed character who is contrasted with two evil characters—Macdonwald, a Scottish rebel leader ('The multiplying villainies of nature/Do swarm upon him', I.ii. 11–12), and 'that most disloyal traitor/The Thane of Cawdor' (I.ii.53–54), who has been fighting on the side of the Norwegian enemy. Duncan, the

Paul Fletcher, "*Macbeth* (c. 1606)," *Shakespeare's Themes as Presented Throughout His Works*. London: Centaur Press, 2002. Pp. 203–11.

Scottish king, praises Macbeth for his performance against the Scottish rebels ('brave Macbeth—well he deserves that name', I.ii. 16), and, when told that Macbeth personally killed Macdonwald, Duncan exclaims 'O valiant cousin, worthy gentleman!' (I.ii.24). (This last praise comes after Duncan has heard that Macbeth ripped Macdonwald open from the stomach to the jaws—'he unseamed him from the nave to the chaps', I.ii.22. It seems that this kind of violence carries Shakespeare's own approval when performed on a rebel.) . . .

The Witches hail Macbeth first as 'Thane of Glamis' (which he is), then as 'Thane of Cawdor', and finally as 'king hereafter' (I.iii.50). . . .

[After inviting the Witches to speak to him, Banquo] is told that, though he will not be king, he will beget kings (I.iii.67). Almost as soon as the Witches have vanished, two Scottish noblemen meet Macbeth to announce that the King has conferred on him the title of Thane of Cawdor which has been stripped from its previous bearer. Banquo immediately identifies the source of the Witches' prophetic knowledge—'can the Devil speak true?' (I.iii.107)—and he goes on to describe them (I.iii.124–6) as 'The instruments of darkness' (i.e., of evil) who tell 'truths' to corrupt human souls ('to betray us/In deepest consequence'). But Macbeth is 'rapt' (I.iii.142), as he was (I.iii.57) after being hailed as 'king hereafter': he is now obsessed with the possibility of his becoming king, and he wonders whether this may entail 'murder' (I.iii.138) or whether it may happen without any action on his part ('Without my stir', I.iii.144). . . .

Power for Her Husband

The coming of Duncan to Macbeth's castle as a guest (Lady Macbeth is informed of Duncan's intended visit in I.v) provides the opportunity for murdering Duncan, and in the scenes I.v to II.iii Macbeth and Lady Macbeth are contrasted in their reactions to evil. For most of this time Lady Macbeth

Glamis Castle, legendary setting of William Shakespeare's Macbeth. Glamis Castle. Reproduced by permission.

is more inclined to evil than her husband. She fears that he is 'too full o' the milk of human kindness' (I.v.15—) to commit murder, and far from needing to be tempted by supernatural forces of evil (as Macbeth was by the Witches) she actually calls on these forces ('you spirits/That tend on mortal thoughts', i.e., are attentive to thoughts about murder, I.v.37–8, 'you murdering ministers', I.v.45) to fill her 'fop-full' with 'direst cruelty' (I.v.39–40).

The Horror of His Acts

When Lady Macbeth appears Macbeth says that they should 'proceed no further in this business' (I.vii.31)—but by the end of this scene Lady Macbeth has won him round. In II.ii we hear that Lady Macbeth's part in the murder was to ply with drink and drugs Duncan's two 'grooms' (attendants)—the nearest Lady Macbeth comes to showing any decent human feeling is her overcoming of an impulse to murder Duncan herself because the sleeping Duncan resembled her father (II.ii.12–13): she has otherwise been completely corrupted by the desire for power. When Macbeth rejoins Lady Macbeth after he has performed the actual murder he is horrified by what he has done. . . .

Immediately after the murder of Duncan [Duncan's] two sons, Malcolm and Donalbain, suspecting that they too will be murdered if they stay in Scotland, flee the country—Malcolm goes to England and Donalbain to Ireland. Macbeth, as Duncan's cousin, is accordingly crowned king. But one crime leads on to another. Macbeth, now that he is king, cannot bear the thought of the crown passing, as the Witches had foretold, to Banquo's offspring. If this happens, Macbeth feels, he has made over his soul to the Devil (by murdering Duncan) all to no purpose (III.i.63–9). . . .

In immediate accord with her husband Lady Macbeth sees the solution as lying in the removal of Banquo and his son Fleance. . . . Macbeth proceeds to arrange for the double murder to be carried out. But this plan, when put into operation, fails to set Macbeth's mind at rest since, during a royal banquet (in III.iv), he is privately informed by one of the murderers that, though Banquo was killed, Fleance escaped, and this information is followed by the appearance of Banquo's ghost. . . .

Learning that Macduff, whom he intended to kill in view of the first apparition's warning, has already fled to England, Macbeth decides out of sheer malice to order the murder of Macduff's wife and children. They are murdered in the scene immediately following (IV.ii). . . .

Result of the Greed for Power

At the beginning of Act V Lady Macbeth is discovered to be in a state of dire mental distress. While sleepwalking she imagines that her hands are stained with Duncan's blood and, whereas after the murder of Duncan she had contemptuously dismissed Macbeth's guilt at the sight of Duncan's blood on his hands ('A little water clears us of this deed', II.ii.67), she now finds that guilt cannot in fact be so easily washed away—now, looking at her own hands, she says (V.i.41–2,49–50): 'What, will these hands ne'er be clean? . . . All the perfumes of Arabia will not sweeten this little hand.' As she recalls the occasions when she tried to allay Macbeth's fears she is now clearly trying to allay her own fears of the consequences of Macbeth's crimes: in particular there is the threat of punishment in hell ('Hell is murky', V.i.30+). Her death is reported soon afterwards (V.v. 16), the result, it is thought, of suicide (V.viii.7.0–1). When Macbeth is told of her death he makes the well-known speech in which human life is dismissed as 'a tale/Told by an idiot' (V.v.26–7): this, of course, is not Shakespeare's own view (as it has sometimes been taken to be), but the view of a demoralised Macbeth. In this last Act Macbeth is 'sick at heart' (V.iii.19) and commands the true allegiance of no one—he observes self-pityingly (V.iii.242–6):

> And that which should accompany
> old age,
>
> As honour, love, obedience, troops
> of friends,
>
> I must not look to have.

His downfall follows swiftly. In Birnam wood the combined English and Scottish forces, led by Siward and various Scottish nobles, camouflage their advance on Macbeth in Dunsinane by carrying before them branches from the wood. Macbeth sees (V.v.43–6) that he has been deceived by the Witches' third apparition, a 'fiend'

> That lies like truth. 'Fear not till
> Birnam wood
>
> Do come to Dunsinane'—and now
> a wood
>
> Comes toward Dunsinane.

And in the battle outside his castle Macbeth is confronted by Macduff, who, Macbeth learns, was not born of woman in so far as he was removed from the womb before time ('from his mother's womb/Untimely ripped', V.viii. 15–16), so that Macbeth (told by the Witches' second apparition that he could not be harmed by any man born of woman) sees that he has again been deceived (V.viii.19–20):

> be these juggling fiends no more believed
>
> That palter with us in a double sense . . .

The play ends with Macduff displaying Macbeth's severed head and with Malcolm proclaiming that as Scotland's king he, 'by the grace of Grace' (V.viii.72), will set the country to rights.

Is Macbeth Solely Responsible?

John Turner

John Turner is a senior lecturer in Modernist and Renaissance Studies at the University of Wales–Swansea. He has coauthored two books on Shakespeare and edited the first folio of The Tragedie of Anthonie and Cleopatra *(1995).*

In the following selection, John Turner observes that most critics think that Macbeth's danger comes from his ambition, which is an aristocratic virtue. But Turner contends that this view seems to ignore the fact that everything one does arises from and is inextricably connected to society. Macbeth is not totally responsible for his actions because his society has made the usurpation of Duncan an exciting challenge, a taboo meant to be broken. The excitement of this defiance places him under a spell; Lady Macbeth, too, is hypnotized by the fantasy of Macbeth as king. Scotland's witches share in the responsibility for the murder, and the pressure he is under makes him vulnerable to his wife's goading and thus able to dismiss what his conscience tells him.

Why does Macbeth kill Duncan? The question may seem simple, but the answer is not, for our whole experience of the play is implicated in it.

Power Turned Against a Country

The motive most commonly given for the murder is ambition. 'The danger of ambition is well described': [eighteenth-century English writer Dr. Samuel] Johnson's judgment is echoed by

John Turner, "Macbeth and Lady Macbeth (I): The Murder and the Motive," *Macbeth*. Berkshire: Open University Press, 1992. Pp. 57–83.

many critics anxious to find a psychological motive in Macbeth that will corroborate their own views of human nature and morality. According to Johnson and the eighteenth-century conservative psychologists behind him, human beings are driven by passions which fulfil their true role only if channelled into a golden mean between two dangerous extremes, and these passions are conceived of as *in* the individual in the same way that the individual is *in* the state. In each case unruliness must be disciplined, and it is one of the functions of literature to help with this discipline.

Clearly, here is a common and fruitful way of approaching Shakespearean tragedy. Each play may be read as the exploration of a potentially valuable aristocratic virtue which has run to seed: ambition in *Macbeth*, jealousy in *Othello*, revenge in *Hamlet*, prodigality in *Timon of Athens*, pride in *King Lear* and *Coriolanus*. In each case an important component of aristocratic honour is turned dangerously against the society it should defend: the passion *in* Macbeth has breached the golden mean, and this in turn has made him a danger *in* the state. Such psychological theory, of course, like all psychological theories, involves a political ideology, and in this case one that would turn Shakespeare's tragedies into morality plays celebrating the harmony of social order: it becomes the business of *Macbeth* to bring ambition to book.

But is this the best way to approach the play? Is ambition a motive in the mind in the same way that a cog is a wheel in a machine? Is the individual an agent in a society in the same way that a machine is an agent in a factory? We must think more closely about this troublesome word '*in*' and the ideological function that it serves. My own view is that it is misleading to separate an individual from his or her society and then to discuss his or her passions as a kind of unruly citizenry. Passions are not simply things within us but relationships that connect us with the world, and it is as relationships that 'they' must be known. We are not simply ambitious, for example: we are ambitious for something. . . .

If motives and passions are thought of as relationships, then the idea of responsibility is immediately complicated: we can no longer separate Macbeth's crime from the social context in which it occurs. It is a tendency of right-wing thought to lay the responsibility for a particular crime upon the individual offender, and of left-wing thought to lay it upon the social context, often challenging a particular society for criminalizing the deed in the first place. *Macbeth* suggests to me that these rival traditions are no more than conventional articulations, for real ends of political power, of what must often remain a mystery; the precise mixture of free agency and predetermined response in human conduct. . . .

Macbeth's Responsibility

So why *does* Macbeth kill Duncan? My own approach will be as follows. When I discuss psychological motivation, I shall speak not of ambition (although clearly Macbeth is ambitious) but rather of malice and envy, for it seems to me that Macbeth is driven not by any picture of himself as king but by the fascinating spell cast by what he knows to be wrong. My own view of him is close to that of [George] Wilson Knight: 'He himself is hopelessly at a loss, and has little idea as to why he is going to murder Duncan. He tries to fit names to his reasons—"ambition", for instance—but this is only a name'. Macbeth is drawn towards the murder in a kind of trance; and when I discuss moral responsibility, therefore, I shall assume that, although he is 'liable to be called to account' for what he has done, he was not 'capable of rational conduct' while doing it. As John Bayley puts it, 'it is essential to the hypnotic tension of the play that Macbeth should not seem in any ordinary way "responsible" for his actions'. In discussing the social context of these actions, I shall trace the origins of Macbeth's hypnotic trance to the double bind imposed upon him by the thought of regicide in his own particular society, leaving him torn between 'I dare not' and 'I would'. His desire to execute the unthinkable is rooted in the ambivalence that surrounds taboo in the 'total' society of Scotland, and thus the whole society of the play is implicated in the strange mystery of his deed. As his metaphors and those of his wife suggest, it involves his relationships in the widest sense. . . .

Harmony in Self and State

In *Macbeth* the human body can be thought of as a text upon which is inscribed the necessity of order to the Scottish body politic. Harmony within the self signifies harmony within the state, division within the self signifies division within the state. Everywhere, in this most physical of plays, we shall find an ideological preoccupation with the body. Hence, of course, the pleasure in dismemberment that the Sisters took earlier in the scene [I.iii.] and hence the new ideology of the body that Macbeth and his wife will try to develop in the scenes ahead.

The man who is rapt, his mind disjoined from his body, is potentially a danger to the state—a danger emblemized for us in the way in which the Sisters suddenly become bodiless and dissolve into thin air. For to be rapt, lost in fantasy, is to be exempt from the disciplines of time and place that Duncan struggles so hard to maintain. Terence Hawkes sees Macbeth's temptation and crime as self-exile from everything, embodied in the rhythms and patterns of Duncan's speech—'an accepted scheme of things, an established world-view, an achieved and authenticated community'—and the signs of this self-exile are everywhere in the rhythms and patterns of Macbeth's own speech. One sign is his neglect of the courtesies that he owes to his fellows, and another is his proneness to soliloquy. In each case, he prefers the private to the public sphere, the individual to the collective; and hence his dangerousness to Scotland. . . .

The Fantasy of Greatness

[Both Macbeth's and Lady Macbeth's] aristocratic understanding of 'greatness' is crucial . . . for it discloses the public source of the most private fantasies of Macbeth and his wife. It is a common paradox that the most private thing in our lives—the imagery of our fantasies—is in fact the most public, precisely because it is an imagery that has come to us from outside, has not been meditated upon and thus has not been integrated into our experience. The twofold fantasy that excites Lady Macbeth is in the air of Duncan's Scotland, barely restrained by taboo: that her husband should be king and that he should become so by murder. Hence her determination to reconstitute the meaning of greatness by separating highness from holiness—the holiness that keeps Duncan high and her husband low—and hence this self-conjuring in her first soliloquy, until her sense of time dissolves and Macbeth seems crowned already (I.v.30). . . .

Macbeth's Immoral Drive

Macbeth's soliloquy in I.vii begins in the equivocal rhythms and the tortuous conditional tenses of a man attempting the same fantastic gamble as his wife, but quickly moves to a sense of the gamble's impossibility. A murderous blow may be fetishized but it cannot sever the social ties of the murderer, his connections with time and place: he may dare Heaven but he cannot dodge judgement on earth. Macbeth's conscience is sensitive to the evils of betraying a king, a kinsman, a guest, a good man. He knows that all codes cry out against his planned assassination; even the word itself, still retaining its original sense of the murder of a Christian leader by heathen fanatics, promises his anathematization.

Yet, despite his certainty, there is something disturbing about Macbeth's verse here too: something quite new, hallucinatory, too much upon the stretch. Arthur Melville Clark has described the soliloquy as 'a succession of dissolving views', Marvin Rosenberg as 'a storm of whirling images'. Does not its swirling iconography—virtues pleading like angels trumpet-tongued, pity like a naked new-born babe striding the blast, cherubins horsed upon the sightless couriers of the air—testify to the strain that Macbeth is under? Are not these symbols different from those created by Banquo, as he watched house-martins fly around the castle battlements? They seem more grandiose, more vague, as though Macbeth's world is fast becoming a phantasmagoria of his own desires and fears, a private theatre within whose walls he is estranged both from himself and from the otherness of the outside world.

This estrangement makes him vulnerable to his wife when she enters; and perhaps all the while . . . he was only waiting for her, playing with the luxury of reluctance, toying with his conscience while secretly indulging his fantasy. No matter whether his wife is petulant . . . , or fiercely reproachful . . . , it is striking that, when she calls him a drunken coward and mocks his equivocation, when she appeals to his courage, his manliness and his aristocratic sense of family, he rises almost immediately to the challenge. He lacks the substantial discipline to any other relationship to restrain him. . . .

In this mood Macbeth, if not without misgiving, finally finds himself enabled to disregard his conscience. . . .

Ambition or Lure of the Forbidden?

It is as though Macbeth is casting around for the one single figure that will confer upon him the murderous identity he seeks, but is driven from figure to figure, unable to settle on one. What is his work? Is it Witchcraft, Murther [murder] or Rape? It is a sign both of his own restlessness and of the 'total' society of Scotland that one image of evil should suggest another. As the wife was excited by thoughts of witchcraft, self-mutilation and infanticide, the soldier is excited by thoughts of witchcraft, war and rape. All things under taboo join hand in hand to arouse them; the whole of Scottish society is involved in their crime.

Hence the inadequacy of 'ambition' to account for his motivation; for these lines do not have the ring of what we commonly call ambition. Does ambition usually feel like *that?* Is it usually possessed of so much relish? What exactly *is* he going to perform upon the body of the unguarded Duncan? Yet even as he talks of himself as Murther bent on Rape, the very words on his lips betray him, for they are tied to the other half-world where Nature remains alive, awake. He knows—or would know if attentive to his own language—that to become the figure of Witchcraft, Murther or Rape is to become 'like a ghost', to betray what he believes most essentially human in himself. . . .

The Loss of Order

The shape of *Macbeth* is an unusual one. Its most important event, the murder of Duncan, takes place early in the play, at the climax of the series of night scenes that began in the torchlit feast of I.vii and end in the bleary early-morning light of II.iii. The murder draws its meaning from this night-time context by means of a series of metaphors that relate it to acts of eating, drinking and sex which have passed beyond the socially acceptable into lawlessness. They suggest that the murder is an act of self-indulgence like an eating binge, a drinking bout, a sexual orgy, whose 'morning after' will hang over Macbeth as long as life itself. Lady Macbeth's words will return ironically against her:

> Was the hope drunk,
>
> Wherein you dress'd yourself? Hath it slept since?
>
> And wakes it now, to look so green and pale
>
> At what it did so freely?
>
> (I.viii.35–38)

The social rituals that should promote solidarity, conviviality and continuity in relationship—the rituals that surround eating, drinking and sex—are about to collapse. The will to take overwhelms the traditions of giving that have sustained Duncan's kingdom; and because such self-will is demonized, it comes over the self consumingly, intoxicatingly, ravishingly. Such metaphors show once more how Duncan's murder is not merely the result of one man's ambition but is the culmination of all the temptations under taboo in Scotland. All the desires repressed under Duncan's rule activate Macbeth and his wife as they murder him. . . .

A Kingdom and a King Destroyed

It is the discovery of the 'treasonous malice' (II.iii.132) of Duncan's murder that finally fragments the kingdom. The stormy night and 'unnatural' weather, the panic and suspicion of the thanes, the flight of the sons—not 'dainty of leave-taking' (II.iii.144)—and the confusion of true and false in everything said and done by Macbeth and his wife: all these signal the end of the play's beginning and, in a real sense, its climax too:

> Confusion now hath made his masterpiece!
> Most sacrilegious Murther hath broke ope
> The Lord's anointed Temple, and stole thence
> The life o' th' building!
> (II.iii.67–70)

Macduff's words are the literal truth as he sees it. This *is* the most sacrilegious murder imaginable. In mutilating Duncan's body, Macbeth has confounded the whole harmonious conception of man, nature and God that Duncan had laboured so hard to maintain.

As the whole of the kingdom has been implicated in the motive, so too the whole of the kingdom has been destroyed in the deed. It is indeed a masterpiece, and one which Macbeth will never be able to repeat; and, unless his words are mere pretence, it is a masterpiece whose obscene beauty still haunts him:

> . . . Here lay Duncan,
>
> His silver skin lac'd with his golden blood;
>
> And his gash'd stabs look'd like a breach in nature
>
> For ruin's wasteful entrance.
>
> (II.iii. 111–14)

Here we see Macbeth's dissociation at its height: a highly idealized picture of the murder, followed by an appalled sense of its gore (II.iii.116). Never again will his imagination be so arrested by a deed. From now on it will in a sense be true that he will find 'nothing serious in mortality' (II.iii.93): all his deeds will wear the antic of the grotesque; all his killing will be anticlimax. Yet there is a counter-truth too. . . . Macbeth's most sacrilegious murder of Duncan is about to usher him into an excitingly new and terrible world, in which his disintegration will dare the most exhilarating extremes of experience and draw the contradictions of the Scottish state into a crisis from which it will never fully recover.

Macbeth as Victim

E.A.J. Honigmann

E.A.J. Honigmann, professor emeritus of the University of Newcastle on Tyne, is often referred to as the dean of Shakespeare scholars.

In the following selection, E.A.J. Honigmann takes the view that Macbeth is presented as more sinned against than sinning, that he is not fully responsible for the murders he commits himself nor those he orders others to commit in his drive to achieve and secure the throne. The responsibility lies initially with the witches, who fan the embers of his ambition and who are in league with Lady Macbeth. She is the one with the greater and more virulent ambition; she goads him to commit the murders, in the process betraying her connection to the witches. She seems to place him in a hypnotic trance, questioning his manhood. And she is the one who falsely places all the blame on Macbeth afterward. Honigmann asserts that Macbeth bears less responsibility than a typical villain because his mental suffering and his state of confusion and helplessness seem to make him more of an agent or onlooker. Furthermore, Macbeth has the best lines of the play, including many soliloquies, and thus the audience is able to identify and sympathize with him.

. . . A victim or a villain? Macbeth seems to be both in the murder scene and, though the mixture differs from moment to moment, throughout the first two acts. This impression partly depends upon the flow of information, which the dramatist can regulate as he chooses. The less an audience understands the more inclined it will be to reserve judgement: in *Macbeth*, the opening scenes are so ar-

E.A.J. Honigmann, "*Macbeth*: The Murderer as Victim," in *Shakespeare: Seven Tragedies*. Shakespeare and the Study of Response. Pp. 129–34, 138–45.

ranged that we never know quite enough about the hero's guilt, and he captures our sympathetic attention as it were under cover of darkness. Commentators who translate surmise into certainty consequently distort the spectator's relationship with the dramatic character: clarifying what the dramatist deliberately left obscure they give us either a villain or a victim, and falsify the very nature of their experience.

A "criminal" hero in particular can benefit from the audience's uncertainties. In the opening scenes of *Macbeth* we are made to wonder about the Weird Sisters, their powers, their connection with Macbeth and Lady Macbeth, and Shakespeare artfully withholds the answers. . . . As the play progresses we learn that Banquo thinks them "the instruments of darkness" (I.iii.124), and that they acknowledge spirits as their "masters" (IV.i.63). But their exact status remains undefined, except that they are closely associated with an "unknown power" (IV.i.69). They may be witches, but we cannot take even this for granted. . . .

The mystery extends to their relationship with Macbeth. Dover Wilson assures us that "Macbeth exercises complete freedom of will from first to last." Another critic wrote, more cautiously, that "Macbeth makes no bargain with the emissaries of the powers of darkness; nor are they bargainable. The knowledge offers itself to him: it is, indeed, as he says, 'a supernatural soliciting.' But he is not solicited to the treachery and murder which he commits." . . .

. . . Lady Macbeth solicits her husband on behalf of the Weird Sisters. She does so, it should be observed, by hailing him by his three titles, just like the Sisters:

> Great Glamis! Worthy Cawdor!
>
> Greater than both, by the all-hail
> hereafter!

She continues where they left off. The Weird Sisters strike first, then Lady Macbeth assaults him in his imagination, blow after blow, and her words have an even more fearful effect—so that theirs seems a joint attack, master-minded from afar. And even if not formally "possessed," Lady Macbeth appears to be somehow in league with evil and Macbeth its victim, a fly in the spider's web who struggles mightily but cannot escape.

"Somehow in league" may sound vague, but we must beware of asserting more than we can prove where the Weird Sisters are concerned. Somehow they make contact with Macbeth's mind, even before he sees them: his very first words, "So foul and fair a day I have not seen," suggest their influence, since he unconsciously echoes their earlier chant. And as they somehow give Banquo "cursed thoughts" in his dreams (II.i.8), and can invade the sleeping mind, what are we to make of the dagger that seems to marshal Macbeth to Duncan's chamber a mere thirteen lines later? Another cursed thought, planted in Macbeth's mind to draw him to the murder? All of these impressions work together, suggesting that the Weird Sisters have access to the human mind (Lady Macbeth, Banquo, Macbeth), and can attack Macbeth's directly and indirectly.

Yet these impressions never harden into certitude. Neither the very first scene, . . . nor any other scene proves beyond doubt that Macbeth is just a victim. The dramatic perspective merely inclines us to fear for him. Shakespeare stimulates an anxiety for the hero, before the murder similar to the audience's protective anxiety for Othello, even though Macbeth's intentions are more straightforwardly criminal than the Moor's. . . . Had the audience actually witnessed a scene where "the husband and wife had explicitly discussed the idea of murdering Duncan at some favourable opportunity," we must reply, Shakespeare would not have been able to arouse the required response, the sense that Lady Macbeth exaggerates her husband's guilt. Such a discussion would have left no

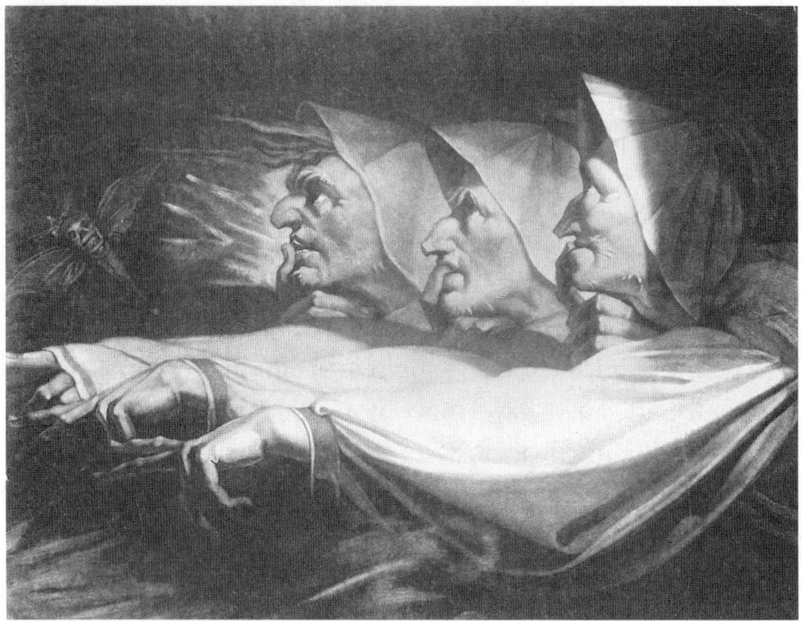

"Three Weird Sisters," depicting the witches from Shakespeare's Macbeth, *by Henry Fuseli (1741–1825), circa 1780.* Hulton Archive / Getty Images. Reproduced by permission.

room for doubt, whereas Lady Macbeth's oblique reference to a previous meeting, in a speech that begins so oddly, exists only to beget doubt:

> What *beast* was't then
>
> That made you break this enterprise to me?
>
> When you durst do it, *then you were a man* . . .

The tendency to overstatement and emotionalism is as marked as, after the murder, her understatement and emotional deadness. Accordingly, though we believe in a previous meeting, we cannot trust her account of it. She *says* that he broke the enterprise to her and swore to carry out the murder, but we have seen how she puts her ideas into his mind ("Hie thee hither / That I may pour my spirits in thine ear") and, though

Macbeth lets her words pass unchallenged, we distrust all that she asserts. Her speech, in effect, makes Macbeth not more but less guilty; we hear her say that he proposed the murder but, not knowing what really happened, we overreact to her emotionalism and think him the more likely to be innocent. . . .

. . . Lady Macbeth later so completely overawes her husband that the first impression is supplanted by a much stronger one. The more she presses him the more reluctant he becomes: and when he finally goes to kill Duncan her hypnotic influence, the vision of the dagger and his "heat-oppressed brain" make him move like a ghost (II.l.56)—a mere ghost of himself, far from exercising complete freedom of will.

Just before the murder of Duncan and immediately afterwards Macbeth impresses us as a victim rather than a villain. The deed is done in horror and, as Bradley has finely said, "as if it were an appalling duty." This is not to claim that Macbeth is simply a victim, only that he seems to be so when it matters most, at the cross-roads of the play, when he feels most intensely, speaks his most moving lines and is most fully himself. And we are given the same sense that he is a victim, it should be noted, by his general way of thinking and imagining. Unlike Hamlet, . . . Macbeth gets carried away by his thought, thought turns into vision, and he himself impresses us as a helpless, horrified onlooker. Just as the sorcerer's apprentice cannot stop the show of kings ("What, will the line stretch out to th' crack of doom?"—IV.i.117) so he cannot halt his imagination once it begins to conjure forth tomorrow and tomorrow and tomorrow, or hounds and greyhounds, mongrels, spaniels, curs, shoughs, water-rugs and demi-wolves. The broken syntax of "If it were done when 'tis done" (I.vii.1–12) also suggests Macbeth's helplessness, a mind bombarded by thoughts that it cannot hold back and yet, in this instance, dare not finish. And his hallucinations have a similar effect. Not only the ghost of Banquo, the dagger, the voices in the murder scene, the hands that pluck at his eyes, the stones that prate of his "where-about": throughout the play mysterious objects and noises float towards him out of the unknown, across the normal boundaries of space and time, always threateningly, so that his characteristic mode of perception also presents him to the audience as a victim, a sufferer who demands the audience's sympathetic response. . . .

Most of the play's defensive maneuvers have been noticed before. Macbeth benefits from an unusual perspective: he speaks all the best verse, he alone engages the audience repeatedly in soliloquy, and in his inward-looking honesty, if not in his speech addressed to others, he represents the play's most sympathetic human value. He appeals to us as his own accuser, so that we can participate simultaneously with his moral and his criminal nature (when the poetry and perspective demand it, in the first two acts). In addition he benefits from minor dramatic stratagems that are less obvious—for instance, the silence of Banquo's ghost (III.iv). Instead of calling for revenge, in the traditional manner, the ghost never competes with Macbeth verbally, which allows Macbeth's point of view to dominate the scene—and to prevail with the audience. . . .

Identifying with Macbeth

Lisa Low

Lisa Low is a Shakespeare scholar and professor of comparative literature at University of California–San Diego.

In the following selection, Lisa Low examines why readers and playgoers empathize with Macbeth in spite of his heinous crimes. Low asserts that Macbeth is pitiable because, like so many people, he "reaches and falls," and he feels remorse for his deeds. Macbeth is able to commit terrible crimes because he suppresses his imagination and his sympathy for others; his actions are enabled by a literal and metaphorical darkness.

As moral obscurity is the world in which Macbeth stands at the beginning of his play, so it is the world in which we are seated watching the play, for the stage is both an extension of Macbeth's mind and the field of our imaginations. . . .

We Identify with Macbeth's Reaching

We identify with Macbeth because the theatre makes us suffer the illusion that we are Macbeth. We pity him because, like us, he stands next to innocence in a world in which evil is a prerequisite for being human. Macbeth is not motivelessly malicious like Richard III or Iago. He savors no sadistic pleasure in cruelty. Rather, set within reach of glory, he reaches and falls, and falling he is sick with remorse.

To have a clear conscience is to stand in the sun. To have a clouded conscience, one hovering between good and evil, between desire and restraint, is to stand where most of us stand, in that strange and obscure purgatory where the wind is pocketed with hot and cool trends, where the air is not nimble and

Lisa Low, "Ridding Ourselves of Macbeth," in *Macbeth*. Edited by Harold Bloom. Major Literary Characters. Chelsea House Publishers, 1991. Reprinted by permission from *The Massachusetts Review*.

sweet but fair and foul. This is the world of choice where thought and act and hand and eye are knit, but in a system of checks and balances.

Set within reach of triumph, who is not tempted to reach? And who, plucking one, will not compulsively and helplessly pluck every apple from the apple tree? For the line dividing self-preservation from ambition is often thin and we walk as if on a narrow cord above an abyss. We have constantly to choose, almost against our wills, for good, for as it is easier to fall than fly, so it is easier to be like Satan than God. We identify with Macbeth because we live in a dangerous world where a slip is likely to be a fall; but in the end, we must rip ourselves from him violently, as of a curse, as of an intolerable knowledge of ourselves. . . .

Failure of the Imagination

Macbeth's damnation comes of a willed failure of the imagination. He permits himself, in spite of conscience, to kill his King. His eyes "wink" at his hands and in that dark moment all cruelties become possible:

> Stars, hide your fires;
>
> Let not light see my black and deep desires.
>
> The eye wink at the hand; yet let that be
>
> Which the eye fears, when it is done, to see.

Conversely, our redemptive victory over Macbeth and over ourselves results from the strengthening of the empathetic imagination which our participation in Macbeth's fall affords. The play restores in us pity which

> . . . like a naked new-born babe
>
> Striding the blast, or heaven's cherubin horsed

> Upon the sightless couriers of the air,
> Shall blow the horrid deed in every eye
> That tears shall drown the wind.

In short, we live and die by our imagination's willingness to comprehend and we comprehend with our eyes. The play is an acting out before our mind's eyes of ourselves participating in and then eschewing evil. . . .

Engulfed by Darkness

If sympathy retards cruelty, empathy prevents it. To be in someone else's skin is to startle at pain, to recoil with human pity from unkindness. Foolish enough to think it possible to commit black deeds and not to be held "to accompt" for it, Macbeth permits his imagination to fail. Considering himself outside his own human skin, Macbeth severs himself. He calls for darkness, commits evil, and is walled-in afterwards in the windowless dungeon of his imagination. A cord yanked from its socket, a chicken with its head cut off, Macbeth shrieks and jerks his way down the corridors of his maimed psyche into death's private cell.

Since cruelty depends upon the imagination's willingness not to see, it is best carried out in darkness. Night obscures witness, prevents the compassionate eye, the organ of pity, the cherub at the gate of sense, from mutinying against the hand. So Macbeth calls for night to cloak Duncan's murder with "Stars, hide your fires," and so he prepares for Banquo's death with "Come, seeling night.". . .

Darkness has its consequences. Once commit yourself to darkness and you are no longer eligible for light's sanctuary. Macbeth calls on darkness to prevent witness to his crime; he wills his eyes to "wink" at his hands, but when he does so, he slits his own wrists and throat. He blacks out.

Shakespeare explores this slitting, this recession into darkness, with physiological metaphors. The cords Macbeth severs—the umbilical one that runs from himself to his kingdom—and the veins and arteries that connect his brain and soul to his body—are the ones which allow him to thrive. Having cut these Macbeth travels through the play as death-in-life—blind, suffocating, stiffening in *rigor mortis*—toward his actual decapitation. Cut off, running beheaded, Macbeth loses internal and external equilibrium. Circulation and communication stop; his body survives, but only briefly, as a body will survive on the impulse of shock, when it has been severed from its head. . . .

[Upon seeing the ghost of Banquo] Macbeth's eyes are as if rolled up into his skull for, dreaming a vision no one in his kingdom can dream, he is far away. Intoxicated, mad, trapped, Macbeth gazes permanently into the bloody narcissus pool of his own mind.

So does Lady Macbeth. She who chided her husband by saying

> The sleeping and the dead
>
> Are but as pictures. 'Tis the eye of
> childhood
>
> That fears a painted devil.

becomes herself a painted devil. Sleepwalking, haunted by her crimes, her "eyes are open . . . but their sense are shut." Like Macbeth's, her mind has closed down around itself, admitting no light, and she sees only the blood upon her hands which for all her rubbing, for all her "out, damned spot[s]," will not rub away. A "little water" cannot clear her of her deeds, nor can she wash the "filthy witness" from her eyes. Instead, the very water with which she tries to rinse her hands free will turn red, proclaiming she is a murderer. . . .

Between Good and Evil

I would like to describe the damned and the redeemed imagination, for we come to *Macbeth* and are entangled, but we leave *Macbeth* released, having learned not what we are, but what we must become.

The imagination is not bound by formal laws of nature. It can pass through walls, enter heaven, drive down into hell. It can make a villain of a hero, and a hero of a villain. When Macbeth stands at the beginning of his play in the fair and foul air of his private thoughts, he is standing between two such large ideas as heaven and hell. As it is heavenly to have new honors sitting upon the brow, so it is hell to stuff the mouth of praise with a dagger. It is hell, too, to be tied to the stake of one ambitious thought until flesh is hacked from bone.

Macbeth stands in the murky, chiaroscuro world of conscience and conscientiousness, between good and evil, a step toward heaven and a slip toward hell. There is but a thinly scratched line between right and wrong, between a sword smoking in a villain's blood and a villain smoking in the blood of a king. Here to "unseam" a man "from the nave to th' chops" may be either a moment of barbaric inhumanity or patriotic fervor. Here if death to the left is laudable, to the right it is enough to throw the self off balance, to push it from its stool and into the blackest abyss of hell. . . .

Macbeth approaches the expressionism to which Shakespeare did not have access. Pressing up against the boundaries of its medium, the play explodes with the pressure of Macbeth's mind. Its language is clotted and heat-oppressed. As Macbeth's mind is "full of scorpions" so is the play's. As [Georg] Büchner's *Woyceck*, [Edward] Munch's *The Scream*, and [Vincent] Van Gogh's self-portraits present minds on the verge of madness, so does *Macbeth*. Shut off from the country of health Macbeth's brain, like a poison bag, distends and bursts, infecting its world. When Ross says,

But cruel are the times when we
are traitors

And do not know ourselves; when
we hold rumor

From what we fear, yet know not
what we fear

But float upon a wild and violent
sea

Each way and none

we recognize that the play occurs inside the upset equilibrium of Macbeth's panicking mind. . . .

Ironic Redeemer

When Macduff reveals himself to Macbeth as the man who not "of woman born" was from his "mother's womb untimely ripped" Macbeth knows what we already know, that though he will fight until his flesh is hacked from his bones, he will be defeated. As Macduff raises his sword he proclaims Macbeth's role for us as redeemer,

Then yield thee, coward,

And live to be the show and gaze
o' the' time.

We'll have thee, as our rarer mon-
sters are,

Painted upon a pole, and underwrit

'Here may you see the tyrant.'

That Macbeth will be the "show . . . o' th' time" puns on the complex emotional effects which drama and visual art have upon us. Beheaded, gored, terrified, and terrifying, Macbeth shall "live" before an audience who shall know through him the true fruit of sin. . . .

When the play is done we shake off the "strange images of death" we have become to be the selves of our hereafter, seeing evil even death, as Macbeth is: dominionless—a gored mask, a painted devil, a head of unfixed hair upon a post.

The Criminal as Tragic Hero

Robert B. Heilman

Robert B. Heilman, University of Washington professor emeritus of English, was chair of the department for two decades and is the author of nine volumes of literary criticism.

The problem pursued by Robert B. Heilman in this selection is how Shakespeare elicits our identification with and sympathy for a man whose ambition for status and power leads him to regicide and to the murder of innocent people, including Lady Macduff and her son. In a classic tragedy, the hero must attain some sense of enlightenment and atonement; Heilman asks whether Macbeth, who achieves neither, can be regarded as a tragic hero. Heilman dissects the various possibilities of that situation, noting that the reader or member of the audience at least partially manages to keep his or her identification with Macbeth, even at the end. Macbeth has almost every characteristic of a tragic hero except for that all-important soul's reckoning. Heilman concludes that, "This is not the best that tragedy can offer."

The critical uneasiness with the character of Macbeth is different from the usual feelings—uncertainty, attentiveness, curiosity, passion to examine, and so on—stirred by an obscure or elusive character, because it springs from a disturbing sense of discrepancy not evoked, for instance, by Shakespeare's other tragic heroes. We expect the tragic protagonist to be an expanding character, one who grows in awareness and spiritual largeness; yet Macbeth is to all intents a contracting character, who seems to discard large areas of consciousness as he goes, to shrink from multilateral to uni-

Robert B. Heilman, "The Criminal as Tragic Hero: Dramatic Methods," *Shakespeare Survey: An Annual Survey of Shakespearean Study and Production*. Edited by Kenneth Muir. New York: Cambridge University Press, 1966. Pp. 12–24.

lateral being (we try to say it isn't so by deflating the Macbeth of Acts I and II and inflating the Macbeth of Acts IV and V). . . .

A Man of Action

[The point to examine] is the mode of our relationship with Macbeth when he kills Duncan; here we have to consent to participation in a planned murder, or at least tacitly accept our capability of committing it. . . . Technically Shakespeare so manages the situation that we become Macbeth, or at least assent to complicity with him, instead of shifting to that simple hostility evoked by the melodramatic treatment of crime. We accept ourselves as murderers, so to speak, because we also feel the strength of our resistance to murder. The initial Macbeth has a fullness of human range that makes him hard to deny; though a kind of laziness makes us naturally vulnerable to the solicitation of some narrow-gauge characters, we learn by experience and discipline to reject these (heroes of cape and sword, easy masters of the world, pure devils, simple victims); and correspondingly we are the more drawn in by those with a large store of human possibilities, good and evil. Macbeth can act as courageous patriot (I, ii, 35 ff.), discover that he has dreamed of the throne ('. . . why do you start . . .?'—I, iii, 51), entertain the 'horrid image' of murdering Duncan (I, iii, 135), be publicly rewarded by the king (I, iv), be an affectionate husband (I, v), survey, with anguished clarity, the motives and consequences of the imagined deed; reject it; feel the strength of his wife's persuasion, return to 'this terrible feat' (I, vii, 80); undergo real horrors of anticipation (II, i, 31 ff.) and of realization that he has actually killed Duncan (II, ii, 14 ff.). Here is not a petty scoundrel but an extraordinary man, so capacious in feeling and motive as to have a compelling representativeness, we cannot adopt him selectively, feel a oneness with some parts of him and reject others;

we become the murderer as well as the man who can hardly tolerate, in prospect or retrospect, the idea of murder. . . .

If it be a function of tragedy . . . to amplify man's knowledge of himself by making him discover, through imaginative action, the moral capabilities to which he may ordinarily be blind, then Shakespeare, in the first two acts of *Macbeth*, has so managed his tools that the function is carried out superlatively well. He leads the leader on to accept himself in a role that he would hardly dream of as his. If it be too blunt to say that he becomes a murderer, at least he feels murderousness to be as powerful as a host of motives more familiar to consciousness. Whether he knows it or not; he knows something more about himself. It may be that 'knows' takes us too far into the realm of the impalpable, but to use it is at least to say metaphorically that the reader remains 'with' Macbeth instead of drifting away into non-participation and censure. Shakespeare's dramaturgic feat should not be unappreciated. . . .

Does Macbeth Feel Remorse?

There may indeed be something of tragic self-knowledge in the man who says that he has 'the gracious Duncan . . . murder'd' and

> mine eternal jewel
>
> Given to the common enemy of
> man;
>
> (III, i, 65, 67–8)

yet he is not saying 'I have acted evilly', much less 'I repent of my evil conduct', but rather, 'I have paid a high price—and for what? To make Banquo the father of kings.' Macbeth is not so simple and crude as not to know that the price is high, but his point is that for a high price he ought to be guaranteed the best goods; and in prompt search of the best goods he elaborates the remorselessly calculating rhetoric by which he inspirits the murderers to ambush Banquo and Fleance. Again, he can acknowledge his and Lady Macbeth's nightmares and declare buried Duncan better off than they, but have no thought at all of the available means of mitigating this wretchedness; the much stronger motives appear in his preceding statement 'We have scorch'd the snake, not kill'd it' and his following one, 'O, full of scorpions is my mind . . . that Banquo, and his Fleance, lives' (III, ii, 13, 36–7). The serpents of enmity and envy clearly have much more bite than the worm of conscience.

I am in blood

Stepp'd in so far

(III, iv, 136–7)

encourages some students to speak as if Macbeth were actuated by a sense of guilt, but since no expectable response to felt guilt inhibits his arranging, very shortly, the Macduff murders, it seems more prudent to see in these words only a technical summary of his poetical method. In 'the sere, the yellow leaf' lines Macbeth's index of the deprivations likely to afflict him in later years (V, iii, 23 ff.) suggests to some readers an acute moral awareness; it seems rather a regretful notice of social behaviour, such as would little trouble the consciousness of a man profoundly concerned about the quality of his deeds and the state of his soul. Finally, in Macbeth's battlefield words to Macduff—

my soul is too much charg'd

With blood of thine already—

(V, viii, 5–6)
some critics have detected remorse.
It may be so, but in the general
context of actions of a man in-

> creasingly apt in the sanguinary and freed from refinement of scruple, there is much to be said for the suggestion that he is 'rationalizing his fear'. . . .

Since different Shakespearians have been able to find in such passages a continuance of genuine moral sensitivity in Macbeth, it is possible that for the non-professional reader they do indeed belong to the means by which a oneness with Macbeth is maintained. If so, then we have that irony by which neutral details in an ugly man's portrait have enough ambiguity to help win a difficult assent to him. However, a true change of heart is incompatible with a retention of the profits secured by even the temporarily hardened heart, and the fact is that once Macbeth has become king, all of his efforts are directed to hanging on to the spoils of a peculiarly obnoxious murder. Shakespeare has chosen to deal not only with an impenitent, though in many ways regretful, man, but with one whose crime has been committed only to secure substantial worldly advantages. . . .

Sympathizing with Evil

The danger point is that at which the admired bravery and its admired accompaniment, resolution (such as appears in the visit to the Witches, IV, i), are distorted into the ruthlessness of the Macduff murders. Here we are most likely to be divorced from Macbeth, to cease being actors of a role and become critics of it. At any rate, Shakespeare takes clear steps to 'protect' Macbeth's position. That 'make assurance double sure' (IV, i, 83) has become a cliché is confirmatory evidence that the motive is well-nigh universal; getting rid of Macduff becomes almost an impersonal safety measure, additionally understandable because of the natural wish to 'sleep in spite of thunder' (86). We come close to pitying his failure to grasp the ambiguity of the oracles, for we can sense our own naiveté and wishful thinking at work; and his disillusionment and emptiness on learning that Banquo's line will inherit the throne, are not so alien to us that Macbeth's retaliatory passion is unthinkable. Shakespeare goes ahead with the risk: we see one of the cruel murders, and the next time Macbeth appears, he is hardly attractive either in his almost obsessive denying of fear (V, iii, 1–10) or in his letting his tension explode in pointless abuse of his servant, partly for fearfulness (11–18). Still, the impulses are ones we can feel. Now, after Macbeth has been on the verge of breaking out into the savage whom we could only repudiate, things take a different turn, and Macbeth comes back toward us as more than a loathsome criminal. He is 'sick at heart' (19)—words that both speak to a kindred feeling and deny that the speaker is a brute. . . .

If then, our hypothesis about the nature of tragic participation is valid, the reader ends his life with and in Macbeth in a way that demands too little of him. He experiences forlornness and desolation, and even a kind of substitute triumph—anything but the soul's reckoning which is a severer trial than the world's judgment. He is not initiated into a true spaciousness of character, but follows, in Macbeth, the movement of what I have called a contracting personality. This is not the best that tragedy can offer.

The Revolt Against Nature and the Father

Robert N. Watson

Robert N. Watson, an English professor and associate vice provost at UCLA, is the author of Shakespeare and the Hazards of Ambition *(1984) and* The Rest Is Silence *(1995), among others.*

In the following selection, Robert N. Watson relates the theme of Macbeth's ambition to fairy tales, especially the Brothers Grimm tale of the fisherman and his greedy wife who lose everything in the end. Macbeth also fits the pattern of Oedipus, the Greek dramatic character who kills his father and marries his mother. In this case, however, the Oedipal image refers to ambition rather than sex. Macbeth, in his rebellion, kills the king, the father figure of the kingdom. The usurpation of the father, a crime against nature, disrupts the divinely intended order of the whole society. The moral that emerges is that the rebellious sons, or subjects, in threatening that order, must be sacrificed.

The crude outlines of *Macbeth* as a moral drama are visible in Elizabethan panegyrics to universal order:

> Now if nature should intermit her course, and leave altogether though it were but for a while the observation of her own laws . . . if the prince of the lights of heaven, which now as a giant doth run his unwearied course, should as it were through a languishing faintness begin to stand and to rest himself; if . . . the times and seasons of the year [should] blend themselves by disordered and confused mixture . . . the fruits of the earth pine away as children at the withered

Robert N. Watson, "Thriftless Ambition, Foolish Wishes, and the Tragedy of Macbeth," in *Shakespeare and the Hazards of Ambition*. Cambridge, MA: Harvard University Press, 1984.

> breasts of their mother no longer able to yield them relief: what would become of man himself, whom these things now do all serve?

A dozen years after Hooker's "Laws of Ecclesiastical Polity" asked these questions, Shakespeare's *Macbeth* provided some fairly conventional answers: man himself becomes a disordered mixture, with no regenerative cycles to rescue him from his mortality and no social system to deliver him from his evil impulses. The cosmic and bodily disorders that accompany Macbeth's rebellion distinctly resemble the ones predicted in the official "Exhortation Concerning Good Order, and Obedience to Rulers and Magistrates":

> The earth, trees, seeds, plants . . . keep themselves in their order: all the parts of the whole year, as winter, summer, months, nights, and days, continue in their order . . . and man himself also hath all his parts both within and without, as soul, heart, mind, memory, understanding, reason, speech, with all and singular corporal members of his body, in a profitable, necessary, and pleasant order: every degree of people . . . hath appointed to them their duty and order: some are in high degree, some in low, some kings and princes, some inferiors and subjects . . . and every one hath need of other . . . Take away kings, princes . . . and such estates of God's order, no man shall ride or go by the highway unrobbed, no man shall sleep in his own house or bed unkilled, no man shall keep his wife, children, and possessions in quietness . . . and there must needs follow all mischief and utter destruction both of souls, bodies, goods, and commonwealths.

In *Macbeth* as in *Richard III*; this deadly loss of personal and natural integrity does not result (as in Hooker) from some careless indolence of the world's ordering forces, but rather (as in the "Exhortation") from a human determination to disturb the political aspect of that order. In murdering the princes who would exclude him from the throne, Richard willingly "smothered / The most replenished sweet work of Nature /

That from the prime creation e'er she fram'd" (4.3.17–19). In unseating Duncan, Macbeth willingly made "a breach in nature" through which "the wine of life" was drained (2.3.113, 95). . . . Both usurpers push back toward primal chaos a Creation that thwarts their desires, hoping to reconstruct it in the image and likeness of their aspiring minds. Ambition, in its inherent opposition to heredity and the established order, thus becomes the enemy of all life, especially that of the ambitious man himself.

But these passages, like most others cited by critics seeking to define a unified "Elizabethan world view," are taken from works expressly written in defense of England's political and theological authorities. Those authorities had a tremendous stake in maintaining order and hierarchy, and in defining them as natural and divinely ordained. If we can recognize in such passages the voice of self-serving pragmatism rather than objective philosophy, we can infer a contrary voice, the voice of the disempowered that the propaganda is struggling to refute. To understand Shakespeare's play, as to understand English cultural history as a whole, requires this sort of inference. The play, like history, like the witches who are agents of them both, "palter[s] with us in a double sense" (5.8.20). Where the witches' prophecies seem to endorse ambition, but warn on a more literal and less audible level against its futility, *Macbeth* contains a silent, figurative endorsement of ambition, even while loudly and eloquently restating the principles expressed by Hooker and the "Exhortation Concerning Good Order."

The spirit of tragedy itself cuts against such single-minded, heavy-handed moralizations, striving subversively on behalf of the individual human will. Shakespeare moves from history to tragedy by clarifying and universalizing the hazards of ambition: this cautionary pattern, which was shaped by the propagandistic aspect of *Richard III*, creates its own sort of moral drama in *Macbeth*. We may view Richard with horrified admiration, but we identify with Macbeth from within, Shakespeare accomplishes this, makes Macbeth eligible for the fear and pity that permit catharsis, by encoding many of our repressed impulses, many of the rash wishes society has obliged us to abandon or conceal, within Macbeth's conventionally dramatic desire to replace the king. In his soliloquy before the regicide, Macbeth acknowledges that his deed will entail all the kinds of violence civilization has been struggling to suppress since it first began: violence between the guest and the host, violence by subjects against a monarch, and violence among kinspeople. When Shakespeare wants to show society's descent into utter deprivacy in *King Lear*, the moral holocaust consists of exactly these crimes: crimes against the host Gloucester, crimes against the royal father Lear, and crimes among siblings over legacies and lovers. . . .

In the history plays, Shakespeare established Oedipal desires as a metaphor for ambition; in *Macbeth*, he exploits the metaphor to implicate his audience in the ambitious crime, by tapping its guilt-ridden urges against authority and even against reality. On an individual as well as a racial scale, the Oedipal patterns psychoanalytic critics have noticed in this play, with Duncan as a father-figure and Lady Macbeth as the sinister temptress who is both mother and wife, may be a way of making the men in the audience intuitively identify with Macbeth's wish fulfillment. For most young men, that Oedipal guilt is a perfect focal point for more general resentments like the ones that turn Macbeth against Duncan: resentments against those who have power over us, those who have things we want, and those whom we want to become. The conflicts Shakespeare is addressing here are not merely the sexual ones. As he demonstrates the deeper meanings and broader ramifications of ambition, he necessarily implies that any desire to change the given order is a scion of that sin; and such a moral inevitably collides with the basic imperatives of life. To live is to change the world, to shape the environment to meet one's

Macbeth, *Act IV, scene I. The Three Witches, Macbeth, Hecat, and apparitions, by Sir Joshua Reynolds.* Public Domain.

needs, even before the Oedipal phase begins, every infant is profoundly involved in a struggle to learn how far that shaping can go, and how best to perform it. So what might at first have been merely analogies or resonances by which Shakespeare suggested the foundations of his cautionary political tales become, in *Macbeth*, the openings through which we enter the story and receive the tragic experience.

To make these openings more accessible Shakespeare expands and details a motif implicit in the history plays' treatment of ambition: the "foolish wish" motif of folklore, in which a person's unenlightened way of desiring converts the power of gaining desires into a curse. Richard III and Henry IV pursue an unlineal, unnatural kingship, and that is precisely what they get, much to their distress. In *Macbeth* this motif acquires the imaginative breadth, and hence the universal applicability, that it has in fairy tales, where it usually involves a narrow-minded disruption of nature's complex balances. The stories achieve their cautionary effect by showing the logical but terrifying ramifications of having such wishes granted. King Midas, for example, acquires the golden touch only to discover that it isolates him from food, love, and family—all the joys of natural life. Perhaps more strikingly relevant to *Macbeth* is the Grimm Brothers' story called "The Fisherman and His Wife." The humble man discovers a magic fish in his net and, at the insistence of his shrewish wife, obliges it to replace their hovel with a castle. The wife steadily increases her demands for splendor and power, the ocean becomes angrier with each new request, and the couple becomes more discontented after each wish is granted, until the fish finally returns them to their original humble state.

But once Macbeth has rashly "done the deed" of self-promotion at his wife's instigation, they both learn that, "What's done cannot be undone" (2.2.14; 5.1.68). Bruno Bettelheim "cannot recall a single fairy tale in which a child's angry wishes have any [irreversible] consequence; only those of adults do. The implication is that adults are accountable for what they do." As such tales fascinate children by providing them with metaphorically coded lessons about the conduct of their own, more basic problems, so *Macbeth* conveys its harsher lessons to us. We do not need magic fish or bloodthirsty witches to provoke us; nature doth teach us all to have aspiring minds, as Tamburlaine asserts, or at least fickle and envious minds. We desire this man's art and that man's scope, with what we most enjoy contented least. Shakespeare alerts us to the fact that, to this extent, we participate in the murderous ambition we witness on stage, creating and suffering its poetically just consequences. While the official homilies claim that rebellion contains all other sins and provokes universal alterations, *Macbeth* suggests reciprocally that all other sins—indeed, all impulses toward change—partake of rebellion.

Foolish-wish stories serve to develop in the child a mechanism and a rationale of repression, a necessary device for subordinating immediate urges to long-term goals and abstract rules—necessary, because infantile desires are no less selfish, violent, and murkily incestuous than the ones propelling Macbeth. Human beings seem to share a stock of foolish wishes, and society survives on its ability to discourage their fulfillment. That may be one reason why the play (as several of its directors have emphasized) suggests that this crisis is only one instance of an endless cycle of rebellion: the play is less the story of two evil people than it is a representation of impulses—ambitious, rebellious, Oedipal—that the hierarchical structures of family and society arouse in every human life. Normal behavior resembles Macbeth's successful curbing of insurrection's lavish spirit early in the play; but deeply human motives constantly impel each person toward a comparable rebellion, differing in scale but not necessarily in basic character from Macbeth's. . . .

. . . In his susceptibility to conventional human desires, and his momentary willingness to forget the reasons they must be suppressed, Macbeth is one of us. He shows us the logical extension, and the logical costs, of our own frailties. Macbeth merely encounters those frailties in a situation that magnifies them into something momentous and horrible; and he encounters them in a dramatic context that blurs the borderline between nightmarish fantasy and reality. . . .

The archetypal crime against the healthy progress of night and day for the Renaissance was also the archetypal crime of filial ambition. Phaethon's disastrous usurpation of Phoebus' solar chariot. Phaethon's premature seizure of his father's place neatly conflated two sorts of rebellion: the attempt to unseat the sun-king, and the Oedipal attempt to take the father's mounts, against his strictest prohibition and before developing the abilities to manage or even survive the attempt. The story's moral is clear enough, and Shakespeare alludes to it to moralize his own cautionary tale: such ambitions, whether they are the seditious ones of a subject or the sexual ones of a son, threaten the universal order by which humanity survives, and the rebel must be sacrificed to preserve that order. . . .

Macbeth Is a Play of Morality, Not Religion

Brian Morris

A former professor of English at the University of Sheffield and a principal of St. David's University College in Wales, Morris served as editor of the Arden Shakespeare series.

In the following selection, Brian Morris notes that Macbeth *is not about religion and that it stresses not the hereafter, but rather morality and Macbeth's place in this world. A consummate soldier in a culture that stresses rank, station, the trappings of power, and warfare, Macbeth is concerned, after Duncan's murder, solely with protecting his position. Macbeth does not worry about his immortal soul. As he degenerates into moral emptiness, he still shows no sign of repentance. To the last, he preserves the strange military image of courtesy combined with personal slaughter, as in earlier action in which he shakes hands with his enemy and then disembowels and beheads him, while still glorying in his own image as a proud and courteous warrior. According to Morris, nowhere else in Shakespeare does this secular mode of piety occur.*

'We cannot imagine him on his knees', says Kenneth Muir of Macbeth, contrasting him with that other murderer, tyrant and usurper Claudius in *Hamlet*. It is a shrewd contrast, since *Macbeth* has little to offer about prayer, repentance, or contrition, though it has much to say about guilt. Indeed, the play is hardly concerned with religion at all. There is no Church, there are no priests, God impinges but slightly on the affairs of humankind. The play is deeply in-

Brian Morris, "The Kingdom, the Power, and the Glory in *Macbeth*," *Focus on "Macbeth."* Edited by John Russell Brown. Andover, Hampshire: Routledge and Kegan Paul, 1982. Pp. 30–51.

volved with the supernatural, with prophecies and portents, with 'Augurs, and understood relations', above all with a piercing analysis of evil, but the other side of the religious coin—sin, repentance, forgiveness, salvation and grace—is no more seen than the dark side of the moon. . . .

Macbeth himself makes this quite clear in I.vii. . . .

If it were done when 'tis done,
then 'twere well

It were done quickly. If th' assassination

Could trammel up the consequence, and catch

With his surcease, success; that but
this blow

Might be the be-all and the end-all
here—

But here upon this bank and shoal
of time—

We'd jump the life to come.

(I.vii. 1–7)

Avoiding Justice

Despite (or perhaps because of) the complex syntactical structure of this passage, with its succession of hypothetical clauses, its repetitions and interpolations, the progress of the thought is analytic, cool and clear. As S.L. Bethell crisply paraphrases it: 'If there were no ill-consequences in this life I should be quite satisfied, for I should ignore the question of a future state.' So, in this speech, Macbeth is content to dismiss death, heaven, hell and judgment from his calculation, and concentrates on the fact that 'We still have judgment here'; this 'even-handed Justice' is the stumbling-block, and his problem is how to circumvent it. He is unconcerned about the *dies irae* ["day of wrath"] and the terrible judgment of God. . . .

[References in the play to] the angels and the cherubim, God's ministers and messengers, are no more than similes and illustrations of the immediate political problem. . . .

This World, Not the Next

Shakespeare presents his hero [as] a man to whom the rewards and terrors of eternity are unimportant. Macbeth, indeed, seems to [as Shakespeare's contemporary, Christopher Marlowe, puts it in his play *The Jew of Malta*,] 'count religion but a childish toy, And hold there is no sin but ignorance.'

This impression is not vitiated by the play's final scenes. When the death of his Queen is reported (V.v), Macbeth is moved to meditate on life and death, but his vision is limited to the earthly realm. . . .

This, as Bethell comments, 'Expresses in Shakespeare's terms the hopelessness of the hardened sinner, to whom the universe has now no meaning', and it 'merely implies the atheism . . . which has resulted from his gradual hardening in crime.' The final scenes of Act V show Macbeth valorous and defiant, but without one whit of concern for his immortal soul.

This is not to deny the presence in the play of what L.C. Knights has called 'images of grace and of the holy supernatural'. . . .

The point is, surely, that the presentation of goodness and holiness in *Macbeth* is muted and peripheral. The tyrant is eventually overthrown by human powers, in hand-to-hand combat, where the presence of God is neither invoked nor declared, though it may be assumed. . . . I would argue that play focuses on the rise and fall of a temporal tyrant, whose religious experience is presented as minimal. Macbeth does not so much oppose God as ignore him. . . .

Macbeth seeks not the kingdom of God but the kingdom of Duncan. . . .

Ambition for Greatness

At the centre of the play's exploration of the nature of power lies the insistence that what is 'high' must be 'holy'. This is not the central thrust of the narrative, nor is it the main course of the dramatic action, but it is the underlying moral truth, and to this extent it is a moral, though not a religious, play.

Although the 'Godlike' attributes of the kingdom, and the power, and the glory are not in the forefront of Macbeth's seeking, in the first three acts of the play we are perpetually conscious of a great drive, onward and upward, an impetus towards some achievement which, it is felt, will provide at least temporary satisfaction of the devouring inner urge. The word traditionally used to describe this aspect of the hero's nature is 'ambition'. . . .

His ambition is not for power, but for status. As we have seen, his desire is not for command over others or for some position from which he can decisively influence the onward course of events, but for personal distinction, recognised and conceded by his society and epitomised by a particular social rank: kingship. This is perhaps the simplest, purest and most naked form of ambition. He does not specifically hunger and thirst after the title and the accoutrements of a king; he simply recognises (instinctively) that a king stands at the top of the ladder, the first link in the great chain, and towards this position of eminence, with the minimum of reflection or meditation, he aims. To use the play's own word, what Macbeth seeks is 'greatness'. . . .

By Act III the gloss has faded, and the central scenes of the play are informed not by ambition for status (it has been achieved), nor by any quest for an extension of 'greatness' (perhaps in terms of pomp and ceremony), but by the restless search for what can only be called 'security of tenure'. The dramatic action swings on that phrase

> To be thus is nothing,
>
> But to be safely thus.

It is not until Act V that we glimpse, and then fleetingly, what must have been Macbeth's vision. . . .

Macbeth dismisses one servant, summons another, and while waiting for him to arrive, says:

> I have liv'd long enough. My way of life
>
> Is fall'n into the sere, the yellow leaf;
>
> And that which should accompany old age,
>
> As honour, love, obedience, troops of friends,
>
> I must not look to have.
>
> (V.iii.22–6)

Honour, love, obedience, golden opinions, these are the concomitants of status, the fruits of 'greatness', and these are the ultimate and only aims of Macbeth's ambition. They may seem few and petty, but Macbeth is neither the first nor the last of Shakespeare's heroes to find that the pleasures of great office lie almost wholly in the imagination of them. A coronation is a climax. . . .

Military Status

Killing the enemy is what Macbeth does best. And at the climax of the play, in the short scenes of Act V, it is personal valour in military combat that characterises his heroic nature; when all else is stripped away it is his essential quality: 'At least we'll die with harness on our back', he says, and 'I cannot fly, / But, bear-like, I must fight the course', and, finally, 'lay on, Macduff'. It is to just such a simple, soldierly intelligence that the idea of status is so attractive. Military life depends upon a hierarchy of command and obedience, a clear, uncomplicated subordination of one man to another; in a word, it depends upon rank. Superior rank, promotion by the correct sequence of gradations, is precisely what the witches offer Macbeth. . . .

Macbeth never attempts to justify his [murder of Duncan] by any appeal to the national interest . . . or the upward thrust of his personal *virtù*. He never claims that he has any right to the throne, nor does he assert that Duncan is a usurper, weak, or in any way inadequate. His clear and undeceived moral intelligence labels the act as utterly evil, and he feels pervasive, dislocating guilt at even the idea of it:

> Than on the torture of the mind to
> lie
>
> In restless ecstasy.

Guilt Without Remorse

The banquet scene, with its fear and confusion—the Ghost of Banquo being seen by Macbeth and the audience, but by no one else—culminates in yet another phantasmal vision of disordered reality, induced by guilt:

> It will have blood; they say blood
> will have blood.
>
> Stones have been known to move,
> and trees to speak;
>
> Augurs and understood relations
> have
>
> By maggot-pies and choughs and
> rooks brought forth

> The secret'st man of blood.
>
> (II.iv.122–6)

All this disables action, vitiates power, and prevents government.

Yet it is guilt without remorse. In the Christian context, as we know from [seventeenth-century writer and preacher John] Bunyan's *Grace Abounding to the Chief of Sinners*, and a host of similar testimonies, the sense of guilt leads to conviction of Sin, and the burden of Sin brings about contrition and repentance, and repentance sues for Grace and forgiveness. There is nothing of this in *Macbeth*. The play remains firmly in the realm of morality and never ventures into the territory where Grace can be the sinner's salve.

Macbeth's Journey into Nothingness

Stanford M. Lyman and Marvin Scott

Stanford M. Lyman, a former professor of sociology at the New School for Social Research in New York, published widely on a variety of topics. Marvin Scott, professor of sociology at Butler University in Indianapolis, has written widely on religion and race.

In the following selection, the authors analyze the play from the viewpoint of existentialism, as developed by Jean-Paul Sartre; that is, the notion that life is essentially absurd, that man defines himself by what he does, and that his existence depends upon choice. For Macbeth, the choice of regicide to achieve power was a bleak decision. He fails to distinguish his initial ambition (the dream of becoming king) from the actions necessary to secure and maintain his position, nor does he consider the inevitable consequences. In awakening to this situation, his world devolves into nothingness and absurdity; he experiences a profound sense of alienation as he moves through forced action and blood-letting with increasing despair. It is a haunting path that is brought to a close only when Macduff ends all action by killing Macbeth and hanging his head on a pike.

Dramatistically . . . the world's a stage, often bloody, filled full with fraud and fragility, a world that unfolds in the ritualistic recurrence of pollution and purification. The dramatistic view of the world, starting in cynicism, leads to a sense of existential despair, a sense of absurdity that most hauntingly finds expression in Shakespeare's *Macbeth*.

This mood of existential despair and absurdity is expressed in Macbeth's tremendous moment of insight:

Stanford M. Lyman and Marvin Scott, *The Drama of Social Reality*. Oxford: Oxford University Press, 1975. Pp. 7–20.

Life's but a walking shadow, a poor player
That struts and frets his hour upon the stage
And then is heard no more: It is a tale
Told by an idiot, full of sound and fury,
Signifying nothing.
(V, v)

Indeed, the entire play is a study of absurdity, with three of its central themes: (1) the sterility of roles divorced from actions; (2) alienation from roles; and (3) meaninglessness of the world whose order is observed only in ritual. By a progressive analysis of these three themes we will uncover Shakespeare's imagery of a world experienced as absurd.

Gap Between Dreams and Reality

There is but one significant action in *Macbeth*—the murder of Duncan. Ostensibly, this murder is committed so that Macbeth can himself fulfill the promise made by the witches and become king of Scotland. Macbeth, however, accuses the witches of being "imperfect speakers." To Macbeth, the system of hierarchy in Scotland is one that divorces role from action, and, thus, he believes that by taking the *title* "king" he will become king. But between being and becoming lies an abyss of action that overwhelms the ambitious thane. Macbeth perceives action as prior to being and thus worries and frets about the state of mind, particular conditions, and immediate problems of *attaining* office. After he attains office, he hopes his life will be as tranquil as the life led by Duncan. But he begins to suspect that the acts he can commit are not self-enclosed and sufficient to his project. He correctly surmises that the relation between being and becoming is not as simple as he had first imagined, that, in fact, being might require permanent attention to the problem of becoming. . . .

Macbeth's terrible self-discovery is that his ambitions are independent of the actions and consequences associated with achieving and maintaining his goals. As Lady Macbeth notes, her husband would be great but without the illness that should attend it. In his soliloquy wherein he debates the merits and risks of killing Duncan, Macbeth hesitates and, with his indecisive meditation, reveals his desire for roles separated from the actions necessary to attain them. . . .

And as Macbeth is ultimately to find out, offices cannot be separated from the actions taken to obtain or to keep them. He has spent his time working up the courage and then devising the plan to seize the throne and, when all should be serene, he must spend the balance of his life defending it. Macbeth is like those princes sorely in need of the advice of [Italian Renaissance philosopher Niccolò] Machiavelli, and, indeed, he lacks the evil *virtu* of [*Richard III*'s] Duke of Gloucester, who claims Machiavellian skills in dramaturgy and who knows the real meaning of the route to royal office. To Machiavelli, being was always an act of becoming, and the latter could never be divorced from the former: Princes who wish to gain and keep the regal ermine must master the arts of show and display, not merely the arts of war, conquest, and *coup* [*d'état*: overthrow].

Ultimately, the absurdity of life is brought home to Macbeth. The witches' bizarre and seemingly impossible prophecy of a wood rising to come against him reveals itself to be a tactic in Malcolm's assault on Macbeth's castle. Macbeth, who has been told that he cannot be killed by man born of woman, is killed by Macduff, who was untimely ripped from his mother's womb. As the darkening clouds of fate descend upon him, Macbeth, hearing of his wife's death, denounces the passing of days as nothing more than time marching at a snail's pace to oblivion. . . .

No Turning Back

And the finale reveals that all has been for naught. The kingdom of Scotland has only been bloodily touched by Macbeth. His murder of Duncan has not secured the throne for him, merely attained it. His actions have aroused the forces of Duncan's legitimate heirs, who, in the end, attain the throne, wipe out Macbeth, and return the kingdom to the *status quo ante* [the way things were before]: Macbeth had intended a creative and definitive act, serving his overweening ambition and bringing about the self-fulfilling prophecies of the witches. He succeeds in the form and fails in the substance of his act. With the accession of Malcolm to the throne, form and substance are reunited, and continuity is restored. But of what are these substances and forms that give order its appearance composed? Malcolm seems to give an answer in the curtain-ringing speech:

> What's more to do
>
> Which would be planted newly with the time . . .
>
> . . . this, and what needful else
>
> That calls upon us, by the grace of Grace
>
> We will perform in measure, time and place:
>
> So thanks to all at once and to each one,
>
> Whom we invite to see us crown'd at Scone.
>
> (V, viii) . . .

Ambition, Alienation, Emptiness

Absurdity—conceived as the ultimate alienation from roles—finds a fundamental expression in the subjective sense that the individual has (1) lost the power to take up routine tasks and to assume offices; (2) lost the capacity to continue actions once carried forth with alacrity and matter-of-factness; (3) lost contact with situations or conditions wherein uniformity and familiarity are to be expected; (4) lost the element of self-recognition to be obtained from acting; and (5) lost the chance to terminate an action once it has begun. . . . Alienation thus fundamentally divorces the actor from his acts and places him in the Camusian situation of exile [referring to twentieth-century existentialist author Albert Camus].

Macbeth's life fulfills most if not all of these conditions of alienation. To understand this we must recognize that the feudal lord obtained his sense of security and identity and fulfilled his role obligations, both routinely and under special cirmumstances, by acknowledging in word and deed his subordination and service to his king. Macbeth acknowledges this early in the drama when, in response to Duncan's praise, he points out

> The service and the loyalty I owe,
>
> In doing it, pays itself. Your highness' part
>
> Is to receive our duties; and our duties
>
> Are to your throne and state, children and servants;
>
> Which do but what they should by doing every thing
>
> Safe toward your love and honour.
>
> (I, iv)

As for his other tasks they are but "labour, which is not used for you" (i.e., Duncan). For Macbeth the routine of his role is secured in the orderliness of the feudal structure, which provides a division of labor, a limited set of actions, and a definite kind of office to each person. Macbeth begins his journey to role alienation by plotting to undermine the very structure that gives his own life meaning and joy.

Once Duncan is dead and Macbeth is king, Macbeth's assumption of his new role proves far more problematic than he had ever imagined. Shakespeare prefigures the problem of Macbeth when he evokes the symbol of the ill-fitting robes with which Macbeth is newly wrapped as Thane of Cawdor. They are "borrow'd robes," as Macbeth first notices, and a moment later Banquo also observes:

> New honours come upon him,
>
> Like our strange garments, cleave
> not to their mould,
>
> But with the aid of use.
>
> (I, iii)

To be king, Macbeth discovers, is not the same for him as it was for Duncan. To protect his sudden rise in fortune, he must murder Banquo and Fleance, Macduff and his family. The normal routines of monarchy are not to be his. Instead, he must steep himself further and further in blood until his evil acts take on a strange and meaningless constancy, losing purpose, redemption, or even the possibility of change when it becomes obvious that they cannot succeed. Early in the drama Macbeth notes the constancy that he can find in the inconstant happenings all around him:

> Come what come may
>
> Time and the hour runs through
> the roughest day.
>
> (I, iii)

Later he confesses to having to go on, to serving the requirements that "blood will have blood," as action takes over for him where intent leaves off.

I am in blood

Stepp'd in so far that, should I wade no more,

Returning were as tedious as go o'er:

Strange things I have in head that will to hand,

Which must be acted ere they may be scann'd.

(III, iv)

Action and Predestination

As Macbeth progresses into evil, he also moves into meaninglessness. He shakes off the familiar and rewarding role of thane but then is unable to assume the seemingly more meaningful and far more desirable role of king. He moves from a condition of humanism, wherein he can connect means and ends and control the consequences of his actions, to one of drift and fatalism. At the last nothing is left but brute action itself, and Macbeth chooses to die in harness as Malcolm's troops move in.

Although Shakespeare is writing a most murderous tale, he reveals a characteristic of the absurd world that [German economist and sociologist] Max Weber, in an entirely different and more benign context, was to discover in the dilemma and resolve created by the Calvinist theology: namely, when the world reveals itself in all its meaninglessness, when purposes are no longer resolved in consequences, when means cannot lead to ends, when projects cannot facilitate plans—men (in all awareness) may plunge into action nevertheless. In pure action alone they hope to find some semblance of meaning and perhaps gain their end after all. As servants bring him word that Birnam wood is coming to Dunsinane, Macbeth at first despairs, and then, like [sixteenth-century French Protestant theologian John] Calvin's Puritan who discovered that God had secretly preordained his election or damnation, he leaps into murderous, blind *action*. . . .

And once started on this bloody, mindless action, he cannot turn back. Macbeth kills Young Siward and observes that the boy was born of woman; a kind of predictability is found in the maelstrom. Macduff appears and reveals that he was not of woman born. The final prophecy now demystified, Macbeth faces a world devoid of hope, possibility, and promise. Offered a chance to surrender he refuses it. Not only does he wish to avoid the ignominy of his defeat, but he also wishes to seize the opportunity for one final and fatal leap into *action*. Action conquers meaninglessness, just as mysterious death fulfills the promise of meaningless life:

> I will not yield,
>
> To kiss the ground before young Malcolm's feet,
>
> And to be baited with the rabble's curse.
>
> Though Birnam wood be come to Dunsinane,
>
> And thou opposed, being of no woman born,
>
> Yet I will try the last: before my body
>
> I throw my warlike shield: lay on Macduff;
>
> And damn'd be him that first cries 'Hold, enough!'
>
> (V, viii)

The Reality of Experience and Despair

When Macbeth has at first become king he expects, or rather hopes, that his new life will find expression in ceremonial activity. But he cannot take the royal seat at table, seemingly the simplest of acts, because the ghost of Banquo, visible only to him, sits there. When finally the ghost relinquishes the seat, Macbeth sits down, but he cannot eat, drink, or enjoy the adulation of the assembled courtiers. The ghost returns and so upsets Macbeth's composure that the banquet must be ended suddenly. Macbeth is suffering quite literally from *dis-ease*, the harbinger of disease, the apprehension that it will be impossible to take up his new role, because the requisite a priori features to taking it up are not present. Moreover, he has burned his bridges behind him. He cannot become thane again. Unable to retrace his steps or to go forward, Macbeth is cast adrift.

Shakespeare likens the loss of self-recognition to confusion of sex roles. Even before Lady Macbeth calls to be unsexed, the images of sexual inversion are foreshadowed in the weird sisters—who are "bearded women." Their sexual inversion betokens an absurd world "where fair is foul" and "foul is fair." Shakespeare attaches the imagery of sexual inversion to Macbeth at the very outset, as he echoes the witches with his first words: "So foul and fair a day. . . ."

In an absurd world words lose their meaning and become the very opposite. And this is concretely symbolized in the confusion found in answering the very simplest of questions posed by *Macbeth*: What is a man? At first Macbeth accepts Lady Macbeth's definition of manhood, which involves *rising* in the world. Ambition is the "gall" that fills Lady Macbeth's breast. Here is the "sticking-place" where Macbeth has come to suck and "screw his courage." So Macbeth believes that a man is one who, unlike animals, can clothe himself—with titles; and if one may *rise* in "the *swelling* act of the imperial theme," he will settle all doubts about manhood. But Macbeth is to learn that his manliness cannot be found in rising to the ultimate manly title: king. Titles, he learns, are as illusory as plays. Unless he can bring forth issue [produce a child], to be king is to be an actor playing a part on a stage. The sterile king is a Player King.

Unable to bring forth issue, he curses the world ("... though the treasure of nature's germens tumble all together/ Even till destruction sickens ...") and lapses into the anguish of a man who cannot locate within himself the meaning of masculine identity. Because he cannot as king bring forth issue, ambition proves to be a false hope that in the end undoes his own sense of manliness. Macbeth comes to learn that—by providing false hope—ambition is like liquor, which makes one "stand to and not stand to." Thus Macbeth's impotence and childlike dependence on female authority highlight the imagery of sexual confusion and epitomize the ambiguities and absurdities of the world. This theme of sex role confusion is returned to over and over as Macbeth in soliloquies and in debates with Lady Macbeth wonders about the sex role appropriate to his plans and deeds. When Macbeth first begins to weaken in his resolve and Lady Macbeth reproaches him for

> Letting 'I dare not' wait upon 'I would,'
>
> Like the poor cat i' the adage

Macbeth replies that

> I dare do all that may become a man;
>
> Who dares do more is none.

But Lady Macbeth points to a different definition of manhood:

> When you durst do it, then you were a man;

And, to be more than what you were, you would

Be so much more the man

and declaims (referring, perhaps, to a child of a former marriage, although poetically even this assumption need not be made)

I have given suck, and know

How tender 'tis to love the babe that milks me:

I would, while it was smiling in my face,

Have pluck'd my nipple from his boneless gums,

And dash'd the brains out, had I so sworn as you

Have done to this.

Nor is she through. Macbeth fears that their conspiracy might fail. Lady Macbeth, who has earlier expressed her concern over the fact that Macbeth "is too full o' the milk of human kindness," and who knows that she must "chastise with the valour of my tongue/ All that impedes thee from the golden round," now lays out in cold detail the entire bloody plan, including how Duncan's guards will be made to appear to be his killers. Macbeth is both fascinated and horrified by her bold ruthlessness. His first remark again recalls the sex-role ambiguity that indicates one element of the meaninglessness that is to come:

Bring forth men-children only;

For thy undaunted mettle should compose

Nothing but males.

(I, vii). . .

Macbeth, *Act III, scene iv. Banquo's ghost, Macbeth, and Lady Macbeth, by R. Westall.* Special Collections Library, University of Michigan. Reproduced by permission.

A Hell of His Own

The last element in our category of "alienation from role" is the fear that, once having undertaken a line of action, one will never be able to end it. The individual feels imprisoned in his role, exercising skills against his own will because he cannot find a way out. Sartre has portrayed Hell as a room, inhabited by disagreeable strangers, from which there is no exit. Shakespeare presents Macbeth's Hell on earth as his inability to escape the murderous course he is set upon. As Macbeth begins to see the dread horror of his predicament, he finds it possible to envy the very man he has murdered:

> . . . better be with the dead,
>
> Whom we to gain our peace, have sent to peace,
>
> Than on the torture of the mind to lie
>
> In restless ecstasy. Duncan is in his grave;
>
> After life's fitful fever he sleeps well;
>
> Treason has done his worst; nor steel, nor poison,
>
> Malice domestic, foreign levy, nothing,
>
> Can touch him further.
>
> (III, ii). . .

But soon the round of murders, attempted murders, and murders yet to be attempted becomes too much. Macbeth begins to see how thoroughly he is ensnared. When told of Fleance's escape from ambush, Macbeth cries out:

> Then comes my fit again: I had else been perfect,
>
> Whole as the marble, founded as the rock,

As broad and general as the casing air:

But now I am cabin'd, cribb'd, confined, bound in

To saucy doubts and fears.

(III, iv)

Soon thereafter the dread routine of his role quite envelops him. He is too steeped in blood to turn back. . . .

To ensure his security, Macbeth must rid himself of all enemies: Macduff, his family, and other possible enemies must be killed. These dread deeds must be done before he is overwhelmed and before his zeal is slowed by reason, deliberation, and hesitancy:

Time, thou anticipated my dread exploits:

Thy flighty purpose never is o'ertook.

Unless the deed go with it: from this moment

The very firstlings of my heart shall be

The firstlings of my hand. And even now,

To crown my thoughts with acts, be it thought and done.

(IV, i)

And, after Macbeth has heard and seen and done so much, he is in despair. With so great an expenditure of blood and fury, dull dread has replaced all feeling, and [no other] death—not even that of Lady Macbeth—can arouse him.

I have almost forgot the taste of fears:
The time has been, my senses would have cool'd
To hear a night-shriek, and my fell of hair
Would at a dismal treatise rouse and stir
As life were in't: I have supp'd full with horrors;
Direness, familiar to my slaughterous thoughts,
Cannot once start me.
(V, v)

And as we have already seen, when the final prophecies of the witches are fulfilled, Macbeth prefers blind action to surrender or suicide. Not even the remembered examples of noble Brutus or cunning Cassius, who died on their own swords, can keep him from the slaughterous action to which his ambition, now more jailer than demon, leads him. Having killed Young Siward, he looks for more victims:

Why should I play the Roman fool, and die
On mine own sword? whiles I see lives, the gashes
Do better upon them.
(V, viii)

And so only Macduff, by cutting off his head, can stop the actions to which Macbeth is now ceaselessly led.

Social Issues in Literature

Chapter 3

Contemporary Perspectives on the Drive for Power

A Modern-Day Macbeth

Somini Sengupta

In 2005, Somini Sengupta was appointed New Delhi bureau chief for The New York Times. *She has won many awards, including the George Polk Award for foreign reporting.*

In the following report on the kingdom of Nepal, Somini Sengupta relates the recent rebellion against the king, Gyanendra, and the government over which he has little control. She describes a past history of royal misuse of power, usurpation, and murder. In 2001 King Birendra and most of his family were murdered in what Sengupta describes as a "gruesome palace massacre." Only the king's brother Gyanendra and his family survived. Gyanendra became the new king, amidst circumstances that point to him as the murderer. Having gained almost unlimited power, one of Gyanendra's many outrages was to suspend civil rights in 2005. In 2006, Communist-led uprisings resulted in the king's power being transferred to the elected government, and Gyanendra's role became largely ceremonial. During those uprisings—in a symbolic act reminiscent of Macbeth's demise—rebels decapitated a statue of Gyanendra's father. In May 2008, Nepal became a republic and the monarchy was formally abolished.

This is the cradle of the kingdom, from where, more than 250 years ago, a shrewd and ambitious king named Prithvi Narayan Shah set off to conquer faraway lands and create the nation now known as Nepal. Here today stands a gleaming white marble memorial in his honor, except that on the pedestal where his likeness once stood, His Majesty's name inscribed below, there is now something decidedly less majestic: a pot of pink geraniums.

The king's statue was toppled by Maoist insurgents [in 2007]. They dragged the head through the narrow cobblestone lanes of Gorkha, smashing it until it broke into pieces and singing, "Long Live the Maoists."

A Monarchy Dismantled

As it happens, the royal past is being dismembered day by day across this onetime Hindu kingdom. Partly it is the handiwork of the decade-long leftist insurgency to overthrow the monarchy. Partly it is the result of public disaffection stemming from the intervention of the current king, Gyanendra, into government.

Whether Nepal will keep some sort of monarchy or scrap it altogether will be formally decided when the country votes next Thursday [April 10, 2008,] for a special assembly to rewrite the Constitution. But as far as the monarchy is concerned, the vote seems largely a formality. It is already being rubbed out of daily life.

A new national anthem makes no reference of allegiance to the king. He no longer heads the army. Pictures of Gyanendra, which once hung in every government office, now gather cobwebs in dank warehouses. The word "Royal" has been dropped from the name of the national airline. Several palaces have been taken over by the government.

[In] December [2007], Parliament voted to declare the country a federal democratic republic. The king must now pay taxes, though at Hindu funerals mourners must still offer prayers to his ancestors.

Indeed, in a society where the king was once regarded as an avatar [incarnation] of a Hindu god, erasing the royal past is not always easy.

Consider Nepal's new currency. Shortly after the king gave up power in 2006, the government ordered the printing of money, starting with the 500-rupee note, free of the king's portrait. In the new design, developed by the central bank, King Gyanendra's image was replaced by that of the noncontroversial Mount Everest. But the paper on which the new bills are printed, having been ordered long ago, still bears a watermark of the king's face.

Unable to afford new currency paper, bank officials took creative license. They slapped a dark-pink rhododendron on top of the watermark. The king and his bird-of-paradise plumed crown can be seen only if the bill is held up to the light.

Murder in the Palace

The ambivalence toward the king is fed by the circumstances under which he inherited the throne. In 2001, his brother, King Birendra, and most of the royal family, were slain in a gruesome palace massacre. In what many here and abroad considered a suspicious turn of fate, only Gyanendra and his family survived.

In 2005, declaring emergency rule, Gyanendra fired the elected government, suspended basic freedoms and vowed to crush the Maoist insurgents. He did not succeed.

Growing frustration with his rule led to street protests in April 2006, prompting the palace to cede power to the last elected government. Eventually, the Maoists locked up their guns and entered politics. The abolition of the monarchy has been the Maoists' chief demand ever since.

A public opinion poll conducted [in January 2008] by a private firm called Interdisciplinary Analysts found Gyanendra's personal ratings to be lower than those of the country's main political leaders: 2, on a 1-to-10 scale.

Even so, 49 percent of Nepalese said they favored retaining the institution of the monarchy, according to the same poll, which surveyed some 3,000 Nepalese and had a margin of sampling error of plus or minus two percentage points. Critics questioned the poll results, describing the polling firm as pro-palace.

Future of the Monarchy

Exactly how Nepalese regard the monarchy is hard to divine. In a spirited defense of the monarchy, a priest at a hilltop temple here said he prayed for the survival of a Hindu kingdom and urged Gyanendra to come and seek the blessings of the sage, Baba Goraknath, after whom this temple is named, to save his throne. "I don't know if Baba likes Gyanendra or not," said the priest, Ishwar Nath Yogi.

Earlier [in 2008], Baburam Bhattarai, the Maoists' second in command, climbed the steep stone steps to this temple and, bizarrely, offered prayers with his parents. The brothers Yogi gave their blessings, albeit reluctantly.

In the shadow of the temple, a porter named Krishna Prasad Neupane, 48, carried backpacks for foreign tourists. "The king is very rich, and the poor are the ones who carry these loads," he said. "We don't need monarchy any more."

Dhanamaya Shrestha, 53, walking home uphill with a sack of vegetables, said she revered the slain king, Birendra, but not his brother. Even her 4-year-old grandson, she recounted, climbed a stool and tore down a picture of Gyanendra that had once hung at home.

A glimpse into the king's own wishes came from Tika Dhamala, a retired army general and the king's former aide-de-camp. Politicians had misunderstood and maligned the king, he said.

Nepalese, whom he called "innocent" and wedded to tradition, were not prepared for the instability of a Nepal without a king. "I'm feeling very uneasy," he said. "Our society is not in a position to accept a complete type of republic."

The wild card is the extent to which the king has loyalists in the Nepalese Army, and if they will act to save the monarchy.

Madhav Bhattarai, the chief priest at Narayanhiti Palace, the king's headquarters in Katmandu, the capital, was not ready to write off the monarchy either. After all, he said, the election date was auspicious according to the Hindu calendar, and the king of Nepal was endowed with divine powers.

"I don't know what he will do to save his throne," said Mr. Bhattarai, 56. "I know Nepal needs the king's role in some form, ceremonial, symbolic; we need the king one way or the other."

Special powers could not save a statue of Gyanendra's father, Mahendra, whose decapitated likeness, eerily draped with a gray cloth, stands in the lobby of the Nepal Academy, where Mr. Bhattarai has his office.

The statue's head was lopped off during anti-palace protests [in 2006]. It was later found in a dirty river.

The Growing Power of the American Presidency

Matthew Crenson and Benjamin Ginsberg

Matthew Crenson and Benjamin Ginsberg are political science professors at Johns Hopkins University. They coauthored Downsizing Democracy *in 2002.*

In the following viewpoint, Matthew Crenson and Benjamin Ginsberg argue that in the last fifty years, the power of the U.S. executive branch has skyrocketed, especially in the two critical areas of war and the economy. The president is in charge of the national budget, which used to be in the hands of the legislature. In recent decades, presidents have plunged the country into war after war, conflict after conflict, without formal declarations of war. In 2003 Congress gave President George W. Bush the power to wage war whenever he judged it necessary. As one elder statesman put it, Congress gave the president a blank check. The authors conclude that as the power of the presidency has risen, democracy has been diminished.

For most of the nineteenth century, the presidency was an institution on the periphery of national politics. In unusual circumstances, a [Thomas] Jefferson, a[n] [Andrew] Jackson, or a[n] [Abraham] Lincoln might exercise extraordinary power, but most presidents held little influence over the congressional barons or provincial chieftains who actually steered the government. The president's job was to execute policy, rarely to make it. Policymaking was the responsibility of legislators, the leaders of the House and Senate. A few com-

Matthew Crenson and Benjamin Ginsberg. "Conclusion: Upsizing the Presidency and Downsizing Democracy," *Presidential Power: Unchecked and Unbalanced*. New York: W. W. Norton and Company, 2007. Pp. 352–68.

manding presidents, such as Jackson, were famous for their vetoes, but most deferred to Congress and rarely presumed to speak their minds to the nation. It was considered bad form. The annual message on the state of the Union, required by the Constitution and transmitted to Congress in writing, was the principal occasion on which the president had a speaking part in American politics.

Today, however, the president has most of the lines, and the presidency has become the engine of national policy formation, especially where money and war are concerned. We are long past the time when the House of Representatives monopolized the power of the purse, doling out dollars down to the level of petty cash. The president is practically master of the nation's budget. And, while Congress may retain the constitutional power to declare war, the power has not been exercised in sixty-five years. The country's military forces have been engaged in conflicts all over the world, but we never declare war. Before invading Iraq in 2003, President Bush demanded and received from Congress what Senator Byrd called a "blank check" from the Congress, "to employ the full military might of the United States wherever he pleased."

For a generation or more, the power of the White House has grown during Republican and Democratic administrations alike. Congressional investigations, personal scandals, and impeachment may have slowed but never halted its advance. Even as presidential approval ratings plummet, presidential power continues to function and grow. The phenomenon is one of the wonders of contemporary national politics.

The political ascent of the presidency was neither accidental nor inevitable. It was contingent on an intersection of presidential motives, means, and opportunities that began to emerge no later than the early decades of the twentieth century. The *motives* of presidents grew more aggressive as the business of becoming chief executive demanded more drive—

the "fire in the belly" that modern politicians must feel before they dare commit themselves to the rigors of the presidential quest. . . .

If the president's personal ambition proved insufficient for the modern presidency, the functionaries of the institutional presidency, including cabinet secretaries and key members of the executive office staff, are usually prepared to promote their own "presidential" agendas. This has been true especially since the Cold War reorganization of the presidency, which institutionalized ambition by providing the president with a regiment of assistants and associates interested in expanding and using the powers of the office. As [President Harry Truman's secretary of state] Dean Acheson hoped, these associates—the [H.R.] Haldemans, [Karl] Roves, [Donald] Rumsfelds, and [Colin] Powells—can compensate for the fact that not every president is a Franklin D. Roosevelt. Outside the cabinet and White House staff are the backers and investors who have a stake in presidential power. They attach themselves to presidential aspirants to advance particular causes or interests. Their aspirations add to the scope of the presidency's institutionalized ambition. . . .

If executive power were held in reserve for urgent crises, the case for presidential primacy might be more persuasive. But presidents exploit the advantages of their office on a routine basis, often to enact elements of their legislative programs that lack both urgency and sufficient support in Congress. President Clinton, for example, used the power of regulatory review to launch an environmental program that had been blocked in the Congress. President Bush used an executive order to place limits on stem cell research, a decision that pleased religious conservatives but could never have achieved majority support in the House and Senate. Right or wrong, these decisions were hardly responses to national emergencies. In both instances, the president was simply asserting his policy preferences and using his executive powers to override or ignore those of his opponents. . . .

But Congress, as we have already suggested, represents a wider range of interests and perspectives than the president, and Congress governs more democratically. Its deliberations are generally open to the public, and its members are not expected to echo the policies of a congressman in chief. True, some members of Congress are venal, inept, or indolent. Incumbents are rarely turned out of office by their constituents. The appearance of public deliberation sometimes masks behind-the-scenes bargains among powerful insiders, and legislative rules sometimes allow entrenched minorities to prevail against the interests of the general public. At its core, however, congressional policymaking operates through open hearings, public debate and vigorous contention among disparate groups. In those rare instances when congressional hearings are closed, it is usually because executive branch witnesses cite national security concerns. Not only are most hearings open to public scrutiny, but members of the public, along with corporations, interest groups, and administrative agencies, have an opportunity to testify. Floor debate, especially in the Senate, can be lengthy and rancorous, and it is by no means an empty exercise in either house. Amendments are frequently offered from the floor and increasingly likely to win acceptance. In short, despite its many imperfections, the U.S. Congress is a democratic decision-making body.

Presidential decision making, on the other hand, takes place in private and often in secret. . . .

The Rise of the Presidency and the Waning of American Democracy

The expansion of presidential power is both symptom and source of an ongoing decay in America's democratic processes.

It is a symptom of that decay because the decline of popular political involvement weakens the Congress and strengthens the presidency. Congressional influence depends on a politically engaged and active civil society. Once elected, presidents only occasionally need such support. In command of armies and bureaucracies, the president can govern according to his own lights, so long as mobilized constituents do not enable Congress to interfere. Contemporary America, with its weak political parties, its partially demobilized electorate, and its citizens transformed into mere "customers" of government, is made to order for presidentialism.

At the same time, the expansion of presidential power is itself a source of democratic decay, because presidents diminish American democracy by being presidential. When presidents rule by decree in even the most routine matters, they diminish democracy. When they and their subordinates ignore, circumvent, and express disdain for legislative processes, they diminish democracy. When they create decision-making processes designed to mute debate and discussion in order to enhance their own power, presidents diminish democracy. In these ways, the onward march of presidentialism makes citizenship superfluous and contributes to what we have elsewhere called the "downsizing" of democracy in America. . . .

The Power of American Dynasties at the Expense of Democracy

Kevin Phillips

Kevin Phillips, a writer and political commentator, contributes to the Los Angeles Times, *National Public Radio, and Bill Moyers's PBS program* Now. *His book* Bad Money: Reckless Finances, Failed Politics, and the Global Crisis of American Capitalism *was published in 2008.*

Using as a background the politics of the late twentieth and early twenty-first centuries, Kevin Phillips explores the Bush family's sense of entitlement in terms of a royal restoration. He compares the fortunes of the Bush dynasty with that of the British Stuarts in the 1660s and the French Bourbons in the late eighteenth and early nineteenth centuries. Phillips points out that both the restored Stuart kings in England and the restored Bourbons in France demonstrated certain qualities, traits, and practices that were closely echoed in the George W. Bush administration: secrecy, deceit, unilateral decisions, and a determination to bring back to the government as many faces from his father's leadership as possible, including Dick Cheney and Donald Rumsfeld.

Back in 1960 or 1980, Americans could fairly have observed that *republics* don't restore ruling dynasties; only kingdoms and empires do. However, amid the turn-of-the-century speculation about the United States' becoming more imperial in its culture and attitudes, it is appropriate to consider two especially useful European analogies to the events and psychologies of U.S. politics between 1992 and 2000. The overthrow of George H. W. Bush in 1992, the moral dissatisfaction with his insurgent successor, and the rising drumbeat among conservatives to replace the usurper with the blood heir of the older ruler are about as close as the American Republic is likely to come to a transatlantic version of the English Stuart (1640–60) and French Bourbon (1789–1815) revolutionary dethronements and subsequent restorations.

Restoration Parallels

The following is a very simplified portrait of the basic parallels. Amid widespread political and economic resentment that turned to revolution, King Charles I of England and King Louis XVI of France were eventually executed, in 1649 and 1793, respectively, and were soon replaced by revolutionary strongmen, Oliver Cromwell and Napoleon Bonaparte. Although both were able leaders, Cromwell and Bonaparte became devil figures to out-of-power royalists, and the frequency of war and crisis under their rule wore on increasingly tired nations. Eventually, after Cromwell's death and Napoleon's 1812–15 military defeats, restoration triumphed. The Stuart heir, son Charles II, was brought back to the throne in England, and the Bourbon heir, brother Louis XVIII, in France.

Needless to say, the motivations and convulsions of a twentieth-century republic cannot precisely, or even very closely, match those of kingdoms in earlier centuries. U.S. presidential elections are not guillotines, however sharp the edge of lopsided defeat might feel to a William Howard Taft, Herbert Hoover, or George H. W. Bush. But as we have seen, Bill Clinton became something of a moral devil figure to some 40 percent of Americans, especially churchgoing Christian conservatives. They responded to the stratagems of the Bush faction of the Republican Party to organize a moral and political restoration around the former president's eldest son.

Revealingly, the Bush restoration mirrored some behaviors and mind-sets visible earlier in the Stuart and Bourbon re-enthronements.

Return of Former Advisors

Restoration, of course, has one central impulse: to recover the past. Each time, that has involved a return of the courtiers, cronies, and prejudices of the expelled dynasty, often the very figures that had helped to incite the earlier expulsion. . . . [In the George W. Bush administration] loyalty has counted more than talent—admittedly an abstraction, where politics is concerned—in filling most cabinet and upper subcabinet jobs.

Richard Cheney's selection as vice president—recommended by George H. W. Bush in a summer 2000 conversation with his about-to-be-nominated son—is a case in point. As the Texas-based chief executive of a major oil services corporation, Cheney duplicated rather than complemented George W. in state of residence, intraparty faction, and industrial-sector bias. He brought no constituency outreach. The outweighing dynastic consideration was the historical need to surround a restored monarch with some of his father's skilled counselors. Cheney, who had been White House chief of staff under Gerald Ford (1976) and defense secretary under the elder Bush, headed this list. His role would be to do for George W. Bush what the earl of Clarendon, a principal adviser of Charles I, did for the early reign of Charles II.

To manage twenty-first-century military preparedness and geopolitics, the Bush administration reached back to the final years of the Vietnam War. Donald Rumsfeld and Richard Cheney, as chief of staff and deputy chief of staff, respectively, had presided over the machinery of the Ford White House in the spring of 1975. This was the bitter April when Saigon finally fell to the North Vietnamese, followed several weeks later by the mishandling of the rescue of the SS *Mayaguez*, an American merchant ship seized by Cambodia. If this defining

President George W. Bush in the Oval Office, following his address to the nation declaring that war had begun against Iraq. Photograph by Brooks Kraft. © Corbis. Reproduced by permission.

Vietnam background is extended to include Cheney's prominent involvement in the 1991 Gulf War, it becomes clear that few regimes have chosen top defense strategy teams whose thinking has been so shaped by the experience of old wars and by an anxiousness to wipe away their lingering embarrassments.

Indeed, so many senior appointees in the second Bush administration had done service under Gerald Ford that David Hume Kennerly, the official White House photographer during that administration, told the *New York Times* in 2002, "I feel like Rip Van Winkle. It's like I woke up twenty-five years later, and not only are my friends still in power, they're more powerful than ever."

Still another set of old faces—from Elliott Abrams, in the mid-1980s an assistant secretary of state, to Cheney himself, back then a helpful member of a congressional investigating panel—reflected the family's loyalty to the *alte Kameraden* [old comrades] of the mid-1980s Iran-Contra scandal. George H. W. Bush had pardoned Abrams and several other participants as one of his last acts as president. Several others may nave earned their recommissioning under the second Bush by earlier service in having kept the Iran-Contra stain from seeping under his father's vice presidential door in 1988. Calvin Trillin, writing in *The Nation*, captured the liberal critique in verse:

> So Elliott Abrams (the felon) is back,
>
> And Poindexter's now a big cheese
>
> High level appointments now favor the guys
>
> With rap sheets instead of CVs [curricula vitae, or résumés].

Insistence on Loyalty and Secrecy

In addition to rewarding old loyalists, dynasties are known—the Stuarts and their retainers somewhat, the Bourbons and their retainers more stereotypically—for forgetting no slight and savoring revenge. One sidebar to the rise of George W. Bush has been the steady elimination of old political foes—Jim Hightower and Ann Richards in Texas; Texas Republican state chairman Tom Pauken; House Speaker Newt Gingrich (George W. Bush helped to force him out in 1998, in part as payment for Gingrich's 1990 embarrassment of Bush senior over taxes); Albert Gore, one of the two 1992 regicides; and Senate Republican leader Trent Lott, a [Ronald] Reagan rather than Bush factionalist. Lott's throat was quickly cut in 2002 when his foolish remark about [senator from South Carolina] Strom Thurmond and segregation handed the White House a sharp knife.

Indeed, the Machiavellian Bush role in the eliminations of Speaker Gingrich and Senate leader Lott—both replaced with easygoing, collaborative successors—underscored yet another frequent restoration policy: to rebuild executive (royal) prerogative and influence at the expense of the legislative branch. Well indexed in both Stuart and Bourbon histories, prerogative expresses itself less as a definable program than as a presumption of entitlement, a hallmark of successful reassertion. New assumptions of authority in war making and secrecy and a bent for unilateralism have been to the George W. Bush dynastic presidency what executive privilege and impoundment were to the imperial presidency portrayed by [historian] Arthur Schlesinger in 1974 [in his book *The Imperial Presidency*].

"Secrecy," argued *Newsweek*, "is another old family trait (both [Bush presidents] were Skull and Bones [an exclusive club] at Yale) in vogue again in Washington. Recall Cheney's secret energy task force, the secret detentions of suspected terrorists and a decision by Bush—terribly harmful to professional historians—to keep the documents of his father and other presidents secret."

Drawing Southern Support

As they have moved toward success, restorations have also usually drawn their forces from particular geographic areas, regions where conservatism and traditional religion were most intense. In the British Isles, the dethroned Stuarts found their strongest support in Ireland, Scotland, parts of Wales, and the north and west of England, where rural populations overlapped with High Church Anglicans and Catholics. In France, staunch backing for the Bourbons could be found in the poor and rural arch-Catholic west of France. . . . For George W. Bush, the analogous locus of his restoration was the South, the part of the United States most given to tradition, family, military service, religion (especially fundamentalist or evangelical Protestantism), a rural gentry, and a lingering regional taste for social events featuring kings, queens, and courts.

The southern colonies of the mid-seventeenth century, appropriately, took the royalist side in the English civil war and cheered the Stuart Restoration in 1660. When another attempt at a Stuart restoration failed in the Britain of 1745, thousands of defeated Scottish Highlanders set sail for the American South, settling in the Cape Fear Valley of North Carolina. In 1861, Confederate secretary of state Judah P. Benjamin, himself British-born, had to deny a report that he had approached British authorities about the South returning to the old flag and monarch. It would have been inappropriate, really, had the first American restoration been centered anywhere else.

Corporate Ambition

Arianna Huffington

Arianna Huffington is the co-founder and editor-in-chief of The Huffington Post, *a nationally syndicated columnist, and author of twelve books, including* Pigs at the Trough: How Corporate Greed and Political Corruption Are Undermining America. *She is also co-host of "Left, Right & Center," public radio's popular political roundtable program.*

In the following viewpoint, Arianna Huffington writes of the powerful "chieftains" of our present culture—the chief executive officers (CEOs) of immense corporations. She blames the destruction of our economy on their greed and "reckless pursuit of limitless wealth." Huffington asserts that the predations of CEOs would not be "possible without an unholy alliance between the CEO class and their buddies on Capitol Hill." Huntington cites the lavish and destructive behavior of many well-known superstar CEOs and compares their behavior to that of psychopaths and sociopaths who lack a sense of remorse and who are indifferent to the suffering of others. Huntington asserts that "The scandals of Enron, Arthur Andersen, Global Crossing, Tyco, WorldCom, Xerox, Qwest, Merrill Lynch, and the rest have exposed a brutal disregard in the boardroom for the fate of those in the office cubicles or on the factory floor."

"Old truths have been relearned; untruths have been unlearned. We have always known that heedless self-interest was bad morals; we know now that it is bad economics. Out of the collapse of a prosperity whose builders boasted their practicality has come the conviction that in the long run economic morality pays." —Franklin D. Roosevelt, Second Inaugural Address, January 20, 1937

Arianna Huffington, "Clutching Forks and Knives to Eat Their Bacon: How Corporate Sociopaths Loot, Plunder and Pillage—and Get Off Scott-Free—While the Rest of Us Pay for It," *Salon.com*, February 11, 2003. Copyright 2003 Salon.com. This article first appeared in Salon.com, at http://www.salon.com. An online version remains in the Salon archives. Reprinted with permission.

In August of 2002 I received a politely phrased notice from my cable company, Adelphia, addressed to "Dear Valued Customer" announcing that my monthly cable fee would be increasing. The letter explained that, "like other businesses, Adelphia constantly faces increases in operational expenses such as wages, specialized training for our employees, utilities, fuel, insurance, equipment." . . . Missing from the missive? Any mention of another operational expense that no one at Adelphia seemed to happy to discuss. During the unfortunate latter days of his reign, former CEO John Rigas had borrowed $3.1 billion from the company and spread the money around like seed on a sun-scorched lawn. His own lawn, of course—he spent $13 million to build a golf course in his backyard, $150 million to buy the Buffalo Sabres hockey team, $65 million to fund a venture capital group run by his son-in-law, thousands to maintain his three private jets, and $700,000 for a country-club membership. It's a wonder my bill's not going up a million dollars a month. I just hope Adelphia's subscribers aren't also paying for his bail.

In the super-heated nineties we were told repeatedly that the "democratization of capital" and unparalleled increases in productivity would level the playing field and produce unprecedented gains in everyone's standard of living. Well, far from closing the vast gap between the haves and the have-nots, the lunatic excesses and the frenzy of fraud perpetrated by our high-flying corporate chieftains have left America's 401(k)s and pension plans in ruins and more than 8 million people out of work. Meanwhile, despite the much vaunted Corporate Responsibility Act and the highly publicized round up of a few of the most heinous offenders, the awful truth is that the corporate tricksters have pillaged the U.S. economy and gotten away with it. They're still living in their gargantuan houses, still feasting on their wildly inflated salaries, and engorging themselves on staggering sums of stock options, while the rest of America tries to figure out how to rebuild for retirement. Or send a kid to college on a worthless stock portfolio.

Ask yourself, Which America do you live in?

Do you live in a $90 million mansion in Bel-Air like Global Crossing founder and chairman Gary Winnick, financed by the cleverly timed sale of more than $730 million worth of stock in the now bankrupt telecom giant? Or do you have a house like Stephen Hilbert's in Carmel, Indiana, with a personal basketball court that's a full-sized replica of Indiana University's Assembly Hall? (Hilbert—an avid Hoosiers fan as you may have guessed—built the house during his disastrous tenure as CEO of Conseco, an insurance company whose stock dropped off the S&P 500 in the summer of 2002.)

Maybe you prefer to kick back, like former Tyco CEO Dennis Kozlowski, on beautiful Nantucket? Sea Rose Farm, Kozlowski's $5 million island spread, features magnificent ocean views, massive fireplaces, a resident chef, a four-bedroom guesthouse, and two seaside cottages—the cutely named "Sequin" and "Edward Cary"—each valued at an additional $2 to $3 million.

Or maybe you don't even bother with a house. Maybe you live on a yacht like Sakura, the 192-foot, five-deck, $10 million floating mansion owned by Oracle CEO Larry Ellison. Or the aptly named Aquasition, which you took off the hands of former WorldCom CEO Bernie Ebbers after the company he led hid more than $7 billion in losses and scuttled its stock. Or maybe these are just too small-time for you. If that's the case, try out Kozlowski's $25 million, 130-foot historic sloop Endeavour, which costs the Tyco tycoon $700,000 a year to maintain.

Or are you one of those corporate titans who has so many million-dollar residences scattered around the globe that you have trouble settling down? Perhaps you'd rather shuttle between homes on your corporate jet. Or is even that too restrictive? When General Electric's retired CEO Jack Welch got fed up with his fleet of cramped corporate jets, he did what any self-respecting capitalist idol would do. He went out and bought a couple of much larger Boeing 737-700s. His allergy to baggage claim is said to be so extreme that even in retirement GE kept a plane at the ready for his impulsive wanderings. Only after the arrangement was made public in his divorce filings did Welch agree to pay $2 million a year to reimburse GE for the jet and a few other perks.

How do you make the most of a long weekend? Instead of planning a backyard barbecue, do you take off for an afternoon at a beach halfway around the world, say in Fiji or Bora Bora, courtesy of your generous shareholders? Or do you line up a golf date with the president of the United States?

Why not jet off to a sunny spot closer to home like Bermuda or the Cayman Islands? CEOs like Joe Forehand of Accenture and Herbert Henkel of Ingersoll-Rand can go there and still claim they're on the job because their companies are technically headquartered in these centers of high finance with warm tropical breezes and no taxes.

How about a little extra spending money? Are you crafty enough to line up the special kind of financing that netted Bernie Ebbers $408 million in loans? Hey, why bother with a nosy bank when you can just write yourself a check for a few hundred million from your very own corporate kitty, at no or extremely low interest? And if you can't pay it back, maybe your company will let you slide for a few months or years or even forgive the whole thing like E*Trade did with CEO Christos Cotsakos' $15 million loan? After all, you're the boss.

And what would happen if, God forbid, you caught a few bad breaks and were forced out of your job? Are you confident that even if you really messed up and not only lost all the company's money but also lost thousands of other people their jobs, you'd still walk away with millions of dollars in bonuses and options and an extremely generous annual pension payment?

If you answered yes to any of these questions, you live in a very special suburb of America: "CEO-ville." It's a cushy, exclusive enclave that has broken away from the rest of the Republic, where the motto is "Land of the free, home of the offshore tax shelter." The currency is emblazoned with the inscription, "In God and crooked accountants we trust," and the Declaration of Independence includes the phrase: "all men are endowed by their creator with certain inalienable rights, that among these are stock options, golden parachutes, and the reckless pursuit of limitless wealth."

In all likelihood, though, you're living in the other America, the one 99.9999% of the country has to make do with. The one in which a record-breaking 1.5 million filed for bankruptcy between March 2001 and March 2002. The one in which investors have lost nearly $9 trillion since March 2000 and retirement assets lost 11% of their value—$630 billion—over roughly the same period.

How did this divisive and anti-democratic tale of two Americas come to pass? How did the impossibly rich upper crust get impossibly crustier? How did we allow the haves to have so insanely much while the rest of America got stuck with the bill? What did our fearless corporate leaders do to deserve such excessive pay and perks, and severance packages, as they laid off hundreds of thousands of hardworking Americans, and magically made trillions of dollars in pension plans and small investor shareholdings disappear?

Understanding Corporate Sociopaths

It's not just that corporate America corrupted the watchdogs that were supposed to be guarding the public interest by feeding them under the table. While it is true that federal regulators, overseers, accountants, and the corporate boards were only too happy to lick the hands that fed them, corporate corruption will not just be chased away by a better-trained pack of Dobermans.

Most of us live our lives according to a set of generally accepted rules. Some are actual laws, which we may or may not be happy with—who likes paying taxes?—but which we follow anyway. Others are moral conventions governed by our sense of decency. We relinquish our seat to an elderly woman on a crowded bus. We hand back the extra money when a cashier gives us too much change. We don't gamble away our kids' allowance in the office football pool. And although we're ambitious, we don't cheat people just to speed up our own rise to the top.

A small group of Americans isn't happy with this arrangement. Not content to conduct themselves according to a code of fair play that allows more than ample opportunity for hard-working, talented, or just plain lucky people to prosper—even to become very rich—they've created their own set of rules that defy logic, violate basic decency, corrupt commerce, and laugh in the face of the laws and regulations established to protect the rest of us. These are the standards that comprise the Code of the Crooked CEO. It's a code of dishonor that rewards unprecedented avarice with gargantuan wealth and ensures a lifestyle of appalling excess—where "keeping up with the Gateses" means that having too much is never enough.

Whenever gang members mow each other down in inner-city shootouts, we are subjected to endless speculation about the root causes of their behavior. Was it a family breakdown, the absence of a father figure, the scourge of crack cocaine, the rising illegitimacy rate, or the collapse of religious values? Watching the latest installments of Must CEO TV—disgraced corporate execs carted off in handcuffs or robotically taking the Fifth in front of congressional committees—I find myself asking the same question: What led these men (and, Martha excepted, they are all men, though one suspects that behind more than a few avaricious men stand greedy women) to do the despicable things they did?

How could they show such wanton disregard for the well-being of so many? What makes them tick—and what made them into ticking financial time bombs? Perhaps instead of the usual talk-show pundits, it would be more useful to convene a roundtable discussion on the subject featuring Dr. Freud, Dr. Jung, and Dr. Phil. Call it "The Three Doctors."

I'd love to hear what these legendary explorers of the human psyche would make of the likes of John Rigas, Dennis Kozlowski, Bernie Ebbers, Sam Waksal, and those Three Horsemen of the Enron Apocalypse, Ken Lay, Jeff Skilling, and Andy Fastow. Were they, as some armchair analysts have theorized, kids who grew up with no love in their lives, now desperately trying to fill the inner void with money and material possessions? Were they suffering from reckless grandiosity? Grotesque delusions? Sheer madness?

In Without Conscience, renowned criminologist Dr. Robert Hare identified the key emotional traits of psychopaths. Included in what he called "The Psychopathy Checklist" were: the inability to feel remorse, a grossly inflated view of oneself, a pronounced indifference to the suffering of others, and a pattern of deceitful behavior.

Could there be any better example of a person with a grandiose—and sociopathic—sense of entitlement, of feeling that the rules that mere mortals live by don't apply to him, than John Rigas? He thought nothing of "borrowing" $3.1 billion dollars from his shareholders so he and his sons could live like sultans—even though they were already fantastically rich, by anyone's definition, before raiding the company coffers.

If you're wondering what the inability to feel regret or shame looks like, take a good look at Dennis Kozlowski. He may have cost Tyco shareholders $92 billion in market value,

Jeffrey Skilling (center), former Enron CEO, surrounded by Enron Vice President of Corporate Development Sherron Watkin (left) and Enron President and COO Jeffrey McMahon, are sworn in on Capitol Hill, prior to testifying before the Senate hearings. AP Images. Reproduced by permission.

and he may be facing criminal trials for tax fraud and for looting $600 million from the company, but "Deal-a-Day Dennis" refused to let a few unfortunate details like these stop him from shamelessly hosting a lavish and boisterous Fourth of July bash—only one month after his art fraud scheme was revealed—at his magnificent spread in Nantucket and aboard his antique racing sloop.

Whether it was a last hurrah or just excess as usual, Kozlowski spared no expense to guarantee that a good time was had by all. A legion of private security guards protected the cases of vintage wine and other goodies being delivered to the yacht, which sat on a mooring that costs Kozlowski $1.5 million a year. After a sail on the Endeavour, one eyewitness reported that "he cruised back into port at the helm—like he was a conquering hero." Unwilling to try his guests' sea legs further, Kozlowski next conquered a lavish repast at the elegant White Elephant restaurant, from which he watched the island's annual fireworks display. And just to show what a stand-up guy he is, Kozlowski stood a round of drinks for everyone at the restaurant's bar. And why not? It's not like it's his money.

You'd be hard pressed to find a man more willing to play fast and loose with the truth than that indefatigable social climber Dr. Sam Waksal. He didn't just lie about big things like the prospects of FDA approval for his company's cancer drug, Erbitux. No, Waksal lied even when there was nothing to gain from the deceit: he claimed he was 52 when he was actually 54, that he was raised in Toledo, Ohio, when he grew up in nearby Dayton. Either way, he's a middle-aged Middle American, so why the subterfuge?

As for Jeff Skilling, who abandoned Enron's sinking ship with his $100 million stock option lifejacket, he exhibits the psychopath's complete lack of remorse, unable to admit wrong-doing. Instead he continues to insist he "made the right decisions." During the nineties, America fell under the spell of the corporate kingpins, putting a premium on charismatic CEOs who looked good on the cover of Business Week or being interviewed on Squawk Box (although many also mainstreamed themselves with appearances on Larry King or even The Tonight Show). It was the era of the rock star CEO. Time magazine even chose two businessmen—Amazon's Jeff Bezos and Intel's Andy Grove—as its Person of the Year in two of the past five years.

It turns out, of course, that far too many of these preening, pampered, overpaid, egocentric corporate American Idols were good on the tube or glad-handing Wall Street but tended to overlook mundane little things like where to list assets and where to list liabilities on a balance sheet.

The off-the-chart CEO extravagances would be a tad easier to stomach if they had been paid for with money earned as reward for superior performance. But they weren't. Many of these superstar executives were not even good at what they were overpaid to do. In fact, some were downright atrocious—to say nothing of felonious. But however much they ravaged their companies' bottom line, it never seemed to affect their own annual haul.

Consider the case of former Ford CEO Jacques Nasser, who was rewarded with millions in stock and cash despite an awful 34-month reign that left the carmaker's revenue in a nosedive and 35,000 workers out of a job. It's hard to imagine that Ford could have done worse if they'd just made decisions by letting a monkey flip a coin.

In fact, the CEOs' lust for excess has been indulged at the direct expense of the pyramid of workers below them. The very system that the CEOs have taken advantage of depends upon the premise that the other America follows the other code—the one based on laws and morality. The scandals at Enron, Arthur Andersen, Global Crossing, Tyco, WorldCom, Xerox, Qwest, Merrill Lynch, and the rest have exposed a brutal disregard in the boardroom for the fate of those in the office cubicles or on the factory floor.

Against all odds, Kozlowski, Waksal, Rigas, and Fastow are actually being criminally prosecuted. But that doesn't happen very often, because most CEOs and their Praetorian Guard of lawyers, accountants, and advisors are smart enough not to break the law. They don't have to.

The mad stampede of greed that coincided with the waning of the bull market and the bursting of the loony tunes tech balloon would not have been possible without an unholy alliance between the CEO class and their buddies on Capitol Hill. For a small fee, payable at the beginning of each election cycle—some call such fees "political donations"; others, less concerned with semantics, political correctness, and charges of slander, call them "legal bribes"—corporate mandarins can purchase an all-access pass guaranteeing a sympathetic look the other way from our so-called public servants. Sure, for a few weeks last summer, when the WorldCom bomb made them fear for their political lives, our political leaders actually passed a set of reforms. But don't be fooled. Both political parties have a richly vested interest in corporate corruption.

The hustling salesmen known as stock "analysts," and their unindicted co-conspirators, the handsomely attired and blow-dried anchors of the cable business news channels, hardly held CEOs' feet to the fire. Glaring disparities in compensation, along with an all-you-can-eat menu of ultra-cushy CEO perks—golden parachutes, interest-free loans, options with obscene returns—were not only tolerated but winked at. And why should the average American have begrudged the CEOs their fabulous pay packages? After all, we thought they were working hard for their money. When stock prices and corporate values were flying so high, why should small-stake stock punters not believe that high-priced executives were worth their inflated salaries, their personal jets, and their shareholder-funded mansions?

Now, of course, we know the appalling truth.

For Further Discussion

1. Discuss how the politics of Shakespeare's time reflect on the issue of power in *Macbeth.* (*See* Andrews, Holland, and Ackroyd)
2. How do literary references, images, and symbols reinforce the evil of powermongering? (*See* Bradley and Watson)
3. Discuss the conflict of values in *Macbeth* (Christianity vs. militarism, order vs disruption, among others). (*See* Hawkes and Blits)
4. Is Macbeth responsible for his acts or is he psychologically out of control or manipulated by the witches and Lady Macbeth? (*See* Fletcher, Turner, Honigmann, Low, and Morris)
5. Does Macbeth, despite his murderous actions, evoke your sympathy? Why or why not? (*See* Heilman, Morris, Lyman, and Scott)
6. Write an essay on the relevance of Macbeth's pursuit of power and status to current world affairs and politics. (*See* Sengupta, Crenson and Ginsberg, Phillips, and Moore)

For Further Reading

Christopher Marlowe, *Tamburlaine*. Edited by Irving Ribner. Indianapolis: Odyssey, 1974.

———, *The Tragical History of Doctor Faustus*. Edited by Edwin Morgan. Edinburgh: Cannongate, 1999.

William Shakespeare, *The First Part of Henry the Fourth*. In *The Riverside Shakespeare*. Edited G. Blakemore Evans. Boston: Houghton Mifflin, 1974.

———, *The First Part of Henry the Sixth*. In *The Riverside Shakespeare*. Edited by G. Blakemore Evans. Boston: Houghton Mifflin, 1974.

———, *The Life and Death of King John*. In *The Riverside Shakespeare*. Edited by G. Blakemore Evans. Boston: Houghton Mifflin, 1974.

———, *The Second Part of Henry the Sixth*. In *The Riverside Shakespeare*. Edited by G. Blakemore Evans. Boston: Houghton Mifflin, 1974.

———, *The Tragedy of Coriolanus*. In *The Riverside Shakespeare*. Edited by G. Blakemore Evans. Boston: Houghton Mifflin, 1974: 1392–1437.

———, *The Tragedy of Julius Caesar*. In *The Riverside Shakespeare*. Edited by G. Blakemore Evans. Boston: Houghton Mifflin, 1974.

———, *The Tragedy of King Lear*. In *The Riverside Shakespeare*. Edited by G. Blakemore Evans. Boston: Houghton Mifflin, 1974.

———, *The Tragedy of Richard the Third*. In *The Riverside Shakespeare*. Edited by G. Blakemore Evans. Boston: Houghton Mifflin, 1974.

Bibliography

Books

Francis Ferguson — "*Macbeth* as the Imitation of an Action," in *English Institute Essays*. Edited by A.S. Downer. New York: Columbia University Press, 1952.

Stephen Greenblatt — *Will in the World: How Shakespeare Became Shakespeare*. New York: Norton, 2004.

Felix Gross — *The Seizure of Political Power*. New York: Philosophical Library, 1958.

F.H. Hensley — *Power and the Pursuit of Peace*. Cambridge: Cambridge University Press, 1963.

Coppelia Kahn — *Man's Estate: Masculine Identity in Shakespeare*. Berkeley: University of California Press, 1981.

G. Wilson Knight — *The Wheel of Fire*. Oxford: Oxford University Press, 1930.

H.N. Paul — *The Royal Play of "Macbeth"*. New York: Octagon, 1950.

James P. Pfiffner — *Power Play: The Bush Presidency and the Constitution*. Washington, DC: Brookings Institution Press, 2008.

M.M. Reese — *Shakespeare: His World and His Work*. London: Arnold, 1953.

A.L. Rowse — *William Shakespeare: A Biography.* London: Macmillan, 1968.

Theodore Spenser — *Shakespeare and the Nature of Man.* New York: Macmillan, 1942.

Garry Wills — *Witches and Jesuits: Shakespeare's "Macbeth"*. Oxford: Oxford University Press, 1995.

Periodicals

Harry Berger Jr. — "The Early Scenes of *Macbeth*: Preface to a New Interpretation," *ELH*, vol. 47, 1980.

Wilkes Berry and Steven Gerson — "From Tree to Weed: Macbeth's Degeneration," *McNeese Review*, vol. 23, 1976–1977.

Harvey Birenbaum — "Consciousness and Responsibility in *Macbeth*," *Mosaic*, vol. 15, no.2, 1982.

Hannah Bloch et al. — "Under the Gun," *Time International*, October 25, 1999.

Dolora G. Cunningham — "Macbeth: The Tragedy of the Hardened Heart," *Shakespeare Quarterly*, Winter 1963.

Maureen Dowd — "Toil and Trouble," *New York Times*, April 9, 2008.

Elizabeth Drew — "Power Grab: George W. Bush Presidency," *New York Review of Books*, June 22, 2006.

Celia W. Dugger	"Party Leaders Say Mugabe Will Fight On," *New York Times*, April 5, 2008.
David George	"Shakespeare and Pembroke's Men," *Shakespeare Quarterly*, vol. 32, no. 3, 1981.
James J. Greene	"*Macbeth*: Masculinity as Murder," *American Imago*, vol. 41, no.2, 1984.
Patrick C. Hogan	"*Macbeth*: Authority and Progenitorship," *American Imago*, vol. 40, no. 4, Winter 1983.
J.H. Jack	"Macbeth, King James, and the Bible," *A Journal of English Literary History*, vol. 22, 1955.
Sharon L. Jansen Jaech	"Political Prophecy," *Shakespeare Quarterly*, vol. 34, no. 3, 1983.
Ninian Mellamphy	"The Ironic Catastrophe in *Macbeth*," *Ariel*, vol. 11, no. 4, 1980.
Tavia Nyong'o	"Kenya's Crisis," *Nation*, January 28, 2008.
Ann Pasternak	"Macbeth and the Terrors of the Night," *Essays in Criticism*, vol. 28, no. 1, 1978.

Index

D

E

F

G

H

I

J

K